The Cannibals at 110 Livingston Street

By

Francine Newman

ISBN: 1-4033-5538-X (e-book)
ISBN: 1-4033-5539-8 (Paperback)

This book is printed on acid free paper.

1stBooks – rev. 01/09/03

Table of Contents

With Heartfelt thanks to my sister, Carolyn Gottlieb and my brother-in-law, Elias Gottlieb for their never-ending support of my efforts to get to court to clear my name. They supported me emotionally and financially, and without these two in my corner, I might very well have sickened under the horrible, on-going frustration.

My Background

I grew up in Laurelton, Queens.
Daughter of a local doctor
Hunter College B.A.
Teachers' College, Columbia University M.A.
I traveled to Europe, Japan and
East and West Africa, to study education
and health practices as well as governments
and history, to earn graduate credits.
I traveled with Syracuse University, and
Howard University, as well as private travel groups.

High School Teacher 29 years
of Health Education and Physical Education
as a Substitute: at Andrew Jackson H.S., Queens
and John Adams H.S., Queens
and Far Rockaway H.S., Queens
appointed   and JHS 210, Brooklyn
Regular Teacher: and Far Rockaway H.S., Queens
and Forest Hills H.S., Queens

Preface

I am dedicating this book to Dr. Thomas S. Szasz, the author, who has written many books and articles about the Atrocities heaped on people by psychiatrists.

His humanistic approach is wonderful.   He cares about the individual whose identity and medical condition belongs to him, and not to the state.   He rejects labeling of individuals and involuntary hospitalization.

I have become acquainted with people in other fields such as NASA.

Some NASA employees, Roger Boisjoly and Bill Bush tried to alert Congressmen about the faulty seals on the challenger space capsule.   Their warnings were ignored and as we all know, the Challenger blew up and the astronauts on board were killed.

Both Boisjoly and Bush were fired and harassed into professional oblivion.

Earlier, another NASA engineer, Bill McInnis, tried repeatedly to warn NASA officials, and various politicians of the dangers of fuel leakage.

He gave his whole self to this effort, but no one would listen. So Bill McInnis gave up, and committed suicide.

I am dedicating this book to other people who tried to help me, using their particular expertise to uncover and expose the horrors they encountered.

1. Lawyer Gene Crescenzi offered his knowledge of legal machinations and emotional support.
2. Allan Wolper, editor of the SOHO Weekly News, investigated the use of psychiatry as a weapon to crush teacher-whistleblowers, for several years, and commissioned a number of articles, by his staff, and wrote several articles himself. In all of these, he exposed the doublespeak, the lack of due process, the totalitarian procedures, and called for political action, to stop the psychiatric railroading of teachers trying to correct wrongdoing in their schools.

3. Nat Hentoff, the civil liberties expert, who wrote an impressive piece in the Village Voice, questioning the use of psychiatry in the schools.
4. Joe Haggerty, a seasoned journalist who was writing educational exposes in the Village Voice, listened to my plea for press publicity, and investigated, and wrote a very strong, condemnatory article titled NYC, USSR?
5. Leonard Levitt, a NY Post reporter, wrote two articles on the psychiatric gulag at Livingston St, after visiting with my attorney, Joan Goldberg, at her office.

and

Jim Jensen, CBS channel Two, hosted an hour long TV program called Who Owns Your Mind?, featuring John Lombard, Me, and Producer Barbara Gordon interviewing Dr. Isenberg. It was powerful.

My overall aim in writing this book is to expose to public view, the rampant corruption in the NYC Board of Education, and the United Federation of Teachers, Local 2, AFL-CTO.

The totalitarian aspects of Board procedures, are hidden and disguised in the Board's contracts and practices.

Blacklisting, psychiatric-labeling of sane, independent-minded teachers, false charges of unfitness, use of students and faculty to attest to events that never occurred, are common practice.

This book shows that there is no elementary due process in any of the Board's grievance hearings, and that the highest officials in the school system use coercive, tyrannical, unconstitutional tactics to maintain the status quo.

This book shows that many of our politicians willingly remain silent, look away, while fraud and constitution-bashing go on, as policy.

This book shows that many doctors can be as corrupt as any common thug, and they must be questioned and de-licensed when found guilty.

This book can inform, frighten and make aware every American employee, in all kinds of workplaces, especially that a psychiatrist may not be a friendly, caring, advocate, for the employee, but rather may write whatever the employer wants written about an employee targeted for firing.

This book will awaken everyone to the fact that their own doctors may be harmful to their health.

This book shows every American the need for vigilance, questioning, for a watchdog approach to all kinds of imposed rules and regulations, by authority, everywhere.

Truth appears to be the enemy.

Facts seem irrelevant.

Whistleblowers in corporations, in the military, in unions, in the education establishment, and in the political and legal houses, have been and are now being mercilessly attacked, because they are decent persons of conscience. This abuse must stop.

I am hopeful that this book will trigger an earthquake of protesters phoning, writing and visiting the legislatures, and the law enforcement officials, who can indict and prosecute the persecutors.

Other teacher-victims of the Board of Ed's psychiatric railroad.

I am mentioning only these people, some of whom were targeted before me (before 1970) who came to my attention.

1   Evelyn Fennell
2   Ganina Stone
3   Alice Lubitch
4   La Frances Hills
5   Maurice Mendoza
6   Ruth Buck
7   Alfretta Hilton
8   Rosemary Madden *
9   Harriet Greenbaun *
10 Alan Tolin   *
11 John Lombard
12 Thomas Murphy

I am certain that files at the Medical Division of the Board, at 65 Court Street Brooklyn contain the names of many victims of the psychiatric railroading procedures.

* These 3 teachers caved in to the medical division's tactics and asked to be permitted to teach, despite their being <u>ordered</u> to submit to a forced psychiatric exam, and did not fight back.

By caving in they made life for those of us who were trying to expose this unconstitutional abuse more difficult.

They cared only about money, not justice.

I My Hit Lists

I am indicting all of these Board of Ed. Administrators, and their staff doctors, as persons who ran the psychiatric railroad, which was designed to destroy teachers who were trying to report <u>wrongdoing</u> by their bosses.

1) All the chancellors serving from 1970 to the present. From Nathan Brown to those serving after him- They are all rubber-stamps who OK anything a principal sends to them. I particularly cite the following administrators Frank Arricale, a Sup't. whose name appeared everywhere Supt. Rose Schwab Supt. Abraham Wilner Chancellor Irving Anker Chancellor Frank Macchiarola

All of the above lied, wrote false reports, and participated with depraved indifference to the truth, resulting in careers and reputations being wrongfully ruined!!!

The corrupt doctors that I came into contact with, through my own case, and through other cases I was made aware of, at the time.

Dr. Sidney Liebowitz the Board's Medical Director
Dr. Naomi deSola Pool the Board's assistant Medical director
Dr. Arthur Nareff
Dr. Morris Isenberg   *
Dr. Jack Schnee   *
Dr. Salvatore Cinque *
Dr. Barbara Wright   *
Dr. Mark Wallfield   *
Dr. Robert Lazarus   *
Dr. Joseph D. Sullivan
Dr. Martin Rudoy
Dr. William Herzlich

* all were involved in my case
   US73eiv473

II My Hit List

The Politicians listed below either remained deafeningly silent when appealed to, for help, or did the absolute minimum action, such as writing a letter to the Board, and then doing <u>no follow-ups</u> to secure action on the complaints.

Senator Daniel Moynihan
Governor Mario Cuomo
Mayer Ed Koch
State Senator Leonard Stavisky
State Senator Emanuel Gold
Congressman Mario Biaggi
Congressman Steny Hoyer
Congressman Joseph Adabbo
Congressman Benjamin Rosenthal
Congressman Jonathan Bingham
Congresswoman Elizabeth
Holtzman
Congresswoman Bella Abzug
Congressman Jack Kemp
Assemblyman Alan Hevesi
City Councilman Arthur Katzman
City Councilman Peter Vallone
City Councilman Andrew Stein
City Councilman Morton Povman
City Congresswoman Ruth
Messinger
City Councilwoman Karen
Koslowitz

All of these elected politicians did the absolute minimum; They wrote a letter or two and then did nothing at all to follow-up or they asked me to send some proof and they'd do more – but they actually did nothing – while the years dragged on, and a career was being obliterated!

There were a few other politicians approached who <u>did nothing</u> but the names listed above are an excellent sample of the <u>political nothing-ness</u>, the gross defection of duty, to help the constituent who appeals to them!!

The Board's Doctors
(Hired Hit Persons)

1) Dr. Barbara Wright Board of Ed. Staff Physician	She was the <u>first</u> doctor I was ordered to see. She found me to be a pleasant woman, neatly dressed, who answered all questions readily, but who spoke constantly. She was unsure about me but decided to recommend that I see the Board shrink –
2) Dr. Mark Wallfield Board of Ed. Staff physician (A Pediatrician)	My Doctors: 1) Dr. Albert Valicenti Psychiatrist (found me to be completely OK no signs of any psychiatric problems)
3) Dr. Morris Isenberg Psychiatrist	2) Dr. Emmanuel Fisher Psychologist
4) Dr. Jack Schnee Psychiatrist	(found me fit to serve as a teacher) 3) Dr. James E. Shea
5) Dr. Robert Lazarus Psychologist	Psychiatrist (found me to be completely OK – described me as a vital, remarkable
6) Dr. Salvatore Cinque Psychiatrist	woman)
7) Dr. Samuel Prensky Psychologist	These three doctors were ignored; only the Boards' doctors results counted! Only Dr. Pool's, Dr. Liebowitz's, Dr. Cinque's, Dr. Isenberg's, Dr. Schnee's, Dr. Lazarus' and Dr. Prensky's reports were considered.

The board culled out some of Dr. Fisher's report and claimed this as their evidence!!

Chapter One

The Jellyfish Among Us Abound

THE JELLYFISH AMONG US ABOUND

The ocean has always delighted and fascinated me. My family always spent summers at Long Beach and Rockaway so that I was introduced at a very tender age to the joys of swimming, walking along the water's edge, and hopping over the little whitecaps as they danced around my ankles, relentlessly. Riding the waves n toward the shore and feeling that wonderful, weightless, floating feeling as the particular wave lifted and then deposited little, frisky me wherever it was headed, was always a marvelous treat to me, and to my younger sister, and to this very day, I drive to the beach and romp in the water, to relax and unwind.

The fresh, sea air and bright sunshine always make it a perfect way to spend leisure time. I also enjoy lying on the beach, just sunning and watching the tide come in and out. There is a very special rhythm that one detects as an ocean-watcher, and it is awesome when one stops to reflect that this has been going on for millions of years.

The myriad forms of life beneath the waves is also a fascinating reality. The schools of tiny fish that swim around one's feet, and the various kinds of larger fish and crabs and clams that wash up on the sand, or creep up one's leg while napping or slither between your fingers while you and the flocks of frolicking children that are always part of the beach scene, are building sand castles, become a part of one's background – an accepted, marvelous aspect of nature.

Frequently, we step on shiny, gelatin-like blobs of matter, while walking along the beach, and upon further examination, we realize the jellyfish are here again. These bizarre, formless chunks of protoplasm come in various sizes and hues, ranging from very tiny, to a few inches in diameter, and since they are somewhat unpleasant to touch, and slippery when stepped on, most people avoid contact with them. They are essentially harmless, except for the species called the Portuguese Man Of War, which is really a cluster of hundreds of jellyfish with poisonous fluid, all clinging together, which can deposit a stinger in your skin causing an unpleasant reaction and possible infection. I am stressing here the fact that I've always thought that jellyfish were harmless creatures, but during these past three years, I have learned that there is a hitherto unmentioned species of jellyfish, and it can be extremely dangerous, and can even kill, in a manner to be explained later.

Of course, I'm referring to that branch of this primitive species that assumes human form. This chapter is all about this kind of spineless creature, which abounds everywhere, in families, in offices, in apartment houses, etc. They are everywhere, but unlike the inert, opaque blobs one steps on or around at the beach, they are difficult to recognize until certain specific conditions are present. Unless these circumstances arise, these jellyfish may seem to be fine, upstanding people, living their life roles as men, women, citizens, parents, aunts, uncles, neighbors, friends, colleagues, workers, from every walk of life. Their spinal columns' lack of calcium, their ability to slither, shrink and even vanish into their immediate surroundings, is not immediately visible, until the particular circumstance arises, which will then call forth all the devious methods they have stored in their psyches, to avoid getting involved when trouble comes. I'm referring to trouble of any kind, especially that which is happening to someone else, who may be a total stranger or a close friend or relative.

You have also seen, I'm sure, people stepping around, or over, some luckless individual lying inert, on a sidewalk, curb or floor, somewhere. They seem to be running to catch that bus, or subway train, or to cross the street before the light changes. But, on closer examination, you realize they are running from something and that something is the possibility of having to become involved. By looking or pretending to look the other way, this jellyfish protects himself from having to see what is there – a fellow human being, in need of a helping hand, or word, or gesture.

The jellyfish person is solely concerned with himself and his own immediate well-being. He lacks empathy, which forces the person to place himself in the unfortunate person's place and feel the pain and woes of the victim, and therefore doesn't offer assistance of any kind.

The jellyfish flees, or pretends hearing loss or faulty vision. It is a deliberate posture and attitude this person assumes. And there is only one underlying reason – fear.

This is my conclusion, based on bitter personal experience at Far Rockaway High School, at U.F.T. high school monthly committee meetings, and from conversations with various acquaintances, friends, and relatives.

Before this nightmare began, I had never given much thought to jellyfish, or cowardice, in its many disguises, or why so few people ever stop to help someone in distress on the street, for example.

The past three years have forced me to reflect on the mass desertion I experienced at the hands of more than 150 teachers with whom I worked and socialized for 16 years. The total silence of the Far Rockaway High School faculty the past two and a half years has been stunning reality.

Not one former colleague ever called or wrote or protested the outrageous unprofessional treatment I had received. Not one former colleague had called to inquire about anything. As an example, in April, 1971, ten months after I was thrown out of my teaching position, Mrs. Gladys Roth, U.F.T. Field Representative handling my case, had to call Bob Arnesen, the Chapter Chairman, to ask him to testify at my "Unsatisfactory Rating" hearing of the Board. Bob was reluctant to appear. He said, "Oh, yes, what ever happened to Fran? What could I possibly do to help her now?" This response from the head of the U.F.T. Chapter, who was supposed to be looking out for the teachers' interests, also knew all the facts of the case from the very beginning. Can you imagine how I felt when I heard his comments? In addition to his rottenness, his co-chapter chairman, Abe Gerewitz, also expressed reluctance to appear, in my behalf, but did consent to attend anyway. Their testimony, as it later turned out, was told in a weak, apologetic manner, and did more for Mr. Gordon than for me. Both Bob and Abe spoke in a hesitant, low, voice, and clearly showed their discomfort at being present at this hearing. Although they were supposed to be testifying for me, as witnesses, to Mr. Gordon's announced intentions of having me ousted from my teaching position, no matter what he had to do to make it happen, their squirming and sniveling kind of testimony made no impression on the two hearing officers. Both these officers were high school principals, Mrs. Bertha Gordon of Morris High School in the Bronx and Louis Schuker, of Jamaica High School, and they were sitting there, smugly, unmoved by my two star witnesses. With "friends" like Bob and Abe, who needed enemies?

I was only asking to be consulted when a parent or student complained about me. I was only asking that Mr. Gordon hear my side of a complaint, and then decide what actions to take.

I was only asking why so many letters were being written by complaining students, when I failed them, because they broke Mr. Gordon's own rules!

I was only asking if Mr. Gordon placed letters of complaint by students in other teachers' files too, without consulting the teacher first. Was I the only faculty member following the principal's memos outlining marks to be given?

How could all the complaining students and parents be justified in their letters of protest, when, in fact, these letters had been solicited by Mr. Gordon, the principal, with the help of Mrs. Mildred Ashepa, the acting chairman of health education, in order to build up some kind of evidence on which to base an "Unsatisfactory" rating in June?

How could a principal make a fair judgment, if he only heard one side of a complaint?

I was only asking my colleagues to join together to get the answers from Mr. Gordon, their principal, too. I was only asking my colleagues to make sure that their contract and rights were being observed by Mr. Gordon.

The answer I got from colleagues was total silence. Silence can be a cruel reply and taught me a sharp lesson; no one cared a damn about me or the issues; "Me first, and to hell with you" was the teachers' attitude.

These jellyfish clumped together, and avoided me and shunned me, and helped Mr. Gordon set up this whole nightmarish chain of events.

Chapter Two

Susan and Robin:
Two of a kind

SUSAN AND ROBIN: TWO OF A KIND

In January, 1969, the chairman of the health education departments, Bob Rommer, announced that he was taking a sabbatical leave, beginning February 1, 1969 and he was picking Allie Metzger, to be acting chairman of the boys' department and was still contemplating his choice of a woman acting chairman. He told me, when I questioned him about his probable choice, that he had made up his mind to give the assignment to Mrs. Mildred Ashepa. I asked him not to appoint her as I did not trust her, and found her extremely aggressive manner unpleasant and shuddered at the thought of having to be under her control. My experience with her generally, was disagreeable, as I do not respect a teacher who would sign a physician's name, to an excuse note for a substitute teacher. This incident had occurred on the last day of school in June 1968.

When I witnessed Mrs. Ashepa and Mrs. Carol Husten, a substitute teacher in our department, talking about the fact that Mrs. Husten did not have time to get her doctor's signature on an absence-with-pay form and now, the school secretary was saying that Mrs. Husten couldn't get paid, etc., I could hardly believe my ears. Mrs. Ashepa said that she would sign it for her and was asking Mrs. Husten for her physician's name so she could forge it, and the teacher would get paid, and nobody would know and all would be well.

I could not bear watching this, so, as they were discussing the absence form, I blurted out that I wished they would go somewhere else and not do the phony signature bit in front of me, as I could never respect either of them again. They left the office immediately, and so I did not actually see Mrs. Ashepa forge the physician's signature, but the whole incident left a very negative and permanent impression on me.

And now, 8 months later, Bob Rommer was asking Mildred to run the department and the thought of it didn't appeal to me, and I said so.

Since Mildred was one of the most recent teachers to join the department, I suggested to Bob that there were other teachers who had seniority, such as Evelyn Leys, who had been in the department more than twenty years, and Alice Nirenberg who was teaching there when I arrived in 1955. These teachers could easily handle the necessary tasks, and all the members of the department could share the various departmental chores, with them. Bob did not welcome my objection to his choice of Mrs. Ashepa, even though I had mentioned the phony signature episode, and literally told me to mind my own business.

I then told Bob I would go to the principal and object there, too.

A unique arrangement as far as women chairmen being in charge of the girls health education department in a high school existed at Far Rockaway High School, and bears brief mention, at this point. That is, there had never been a licensed woman chairman of the health education at the school. Why this was so I never was able to find out, but the male chairman of the boys' health education department was in charge of both departments, officially, even though a woman teacher helped out in running the department. I had served on various committees within the department and had handled incoming mail, arranged for guests and films for our hygiene program, and had attended professional meetings as the chairman's representative, for several years, and the other members of our department shared equally in the many jobs that kept the department running smoothly.

I asked Bob Arnesen, the U.F.T. chapter chairman, to accompany me to Mr. Gordon's office, so that I could voice my objection to Mildred Ashepa's appointment as acting head of my department. Bob arranged for this conference and we went to see Mr. Gordon, a few days later.

If you've ever locked yourself in a closet or a bank vault, by accident, and found yourself banging on a steel door, with no response or result forthcoming, other than bruised knuckles and a mounting sense of utter frustration, you can appreciate my feelings, both during and after the discussion that took place in this principal's office.

Mr. Gordon sat there, smugly, arrogantly, as I explained why I didn't relish the prospect of working under Mrs. Ashepa's direction, and why I didn't trust her. When I finished speaking, he said that he could choose anyone he wanted, it was his prerogative as principal, and that he was not the least bit interested in my feelings and objections. What was particularly unfair here is that he also said that he hadn't seen Mrs. Ashepa forge the medical and therefore as far as he was concerned, the incident had not taken place.

I shivered with revulsion, at the attitude of this man, and then stated my second reason for asking for this meeting, and although I imagine that the reader might imagine that Mr. Gordon's response to my second statement and request might contain a tinge of warmth or empathy, let me dispel any such thought from your consciousness right here. As I told him, painfully, that my mother was gravely ill with a diagnosed irreversible brain tumor, and might die at any moment, there was no change of expression on his frozen features. I continued with a request that I be called to the nearest phone immediately, if a call came to the school for me, and that this special circumstance should be enough to dispense with the usual red tape of placing phone messages in letter boxes, rather than delivering them to the teacher, at once, in case the message was very urgent, demanding the teacher's immediate acknowledgement. My last point was to inform the principal that I might have to be absent for a week or longer when this inevitable event occurred, and I wanted him, as head of the school, to know why I was absent, but that I did not care to have my private grief tacked up on the faculty bulletin board, to be a gossip item.

Bob Arnesen offered his arm and made an appropriate statement of sadness at the awful news I had just announced, but Mr. Gordon made it perfectly clear by his coldness and non-verbal communication, that what I was saying was totally unimportant in his scheme of things and would I please leave as the period was about over and he had so many more important things to do.

As I punched out that day, and drove home, I had a feeling of impending doom, as though a cloud had settled over me and besides the daily horror of visiting my mother at the hospital, knowing all the time that she was lying on her deathbed, school was going to be unpleasant with this female know-it-all bossing everyone around. I had no choice except to try to do the best I could at the hospital and at school.

The spring term began, and there was the usual hustle and bustle in the halls and classrooms, as students and teachers ran around trying to find rooms, books, delaney cards, schedules, keys and each other. The usual chaos prevailed for the first 10 days or so, until, eventually, a purposeful quiet pervaded the halls and rooms, as students and teachers settled in for the real things, learning and instructing.

I followed my daily program, meeting my new students, organizing them, interviewing them, as we all interacted, in the classrooms, in the locker room, and in the gym.

While the new term was gradually settling into routine, there were some devices set into motion by the administration to foster efficiency and ensure proper programming and control traffic in the corridors. Teachers were requested to stand out in the halls during change of class, to start classes promptly to cut down on late-comers to class, and to check faculty signatures and I followed them scrupulously, because I believe in a firm and fair kind of approach to handling students. Having rules for the youngsters to follow gives them a sense of what is expected of them, and provides guidelines within which they can operate. If the student follows the rules, gets to classes on time, does his or her work, attends classes that are assigned to him, he or she can feel a sense of achievement in knowing he's doing the accepted, the right thing.

It was in this spirit of following administrative memos to the best of my ability, so that I, too, could have a firm base of efficient handling of my responsibilities, that I was checking signatures on my students' program cards, in my homeroom. This was the third morning in a row that teachers were told to check each signature on the students' program card, and five minutes extra time was added to the home room time, to permit time for careful checking.

Most of my homeroom students were chatting quietly, or glancing at their homework in preparation for classes, when Susan Reiner started yelling at me. "Quit bugging, me, Miss Newman. You better stop picking on me, or I'll make trouble for you. You'll see." I was so startled by her outburst, that I just stood there, dumbfounded. "Susan, you still have two missing signatures on your program card. I'll have to report you to the dean. I've given you the three days allotted for signatures, and after your behavior today, you'll have a bit of explaining to do, about this, too. I will not permit you to speak to me this way, young lady," I told her in a serious tone.

The class was watching the turn of events, with interest. I went to my desk, and filled out a report to the dean on Susan, and the bell rang. I did not know Susan very well, but had not formed any strong impression of her yet, since I only saw her for a few minutes each day in home room. After her nasty display of temper, I could only conclude that she felt guilty about getting caught. She had the same amount of time to check into all her classes as any other student, and the fact that two teachers signatures were still missing, could only mean that Susan was not following school regulations, and might even be breaking them. I turned in the report to the dean, and went on my way.

The next morning I found a note from Mr. Gordon in my letterbox. It was a brief memo, and attached to it was a letter of outrage from Mrs. Reiner, Susan's mother. She demanded that Susan be removed from that nasty Miss Newman's class immediately, or she would take some action, etc. The whole thing was ridiculous. I went into the principal's office, as requested, and told him my opinion of the basis for the letter. "It's obvious that Susan lied to her mother and told her that I yelled at her, when in fact, Susan had not signed into two classes and I followed your directive, Mr. Gordon, and reported her to the dean on the third day of checking. Susan was extremely insolent to me."

Mr. Gordon sat there, impassively, and then said, sternly, "This is a very serious complaint Mrs. Reiner is making. Good day, Miss Newman." Not a word of understanding that I was, indeed, following his directions and that Susan was wrong, and should be disciplined and made to face up to her failure to sign in to her classes. He simply sided with the mother, who was hearing only her daughter's point of view. I was outraged, but resolved to go about my duties and try to forget the despot who was running the school.

The next morning I found another letter from Mr. Gordon. It directed me to appear in Mr. Seiden's office later in the day to discuss a parent complaint. Mr. Seiden was an assistant principal, and since I had always had pleasant dealings with him and thought of him in friendly terms, since he always had a joke or two to tell, I could not and did not fear the meeting, but was rather curious about what might occur.

9

I reported for the meeting and found Mr. Seiden in his office chatting with an attractive woman. She appeared to be agitated, and was gesticulating with her hands.

Mr. Seiden stood up as I entered the room and motioned me to a chair. "This is Mrs. Reiner, Miss Newman." I acknowledged her, and she glared at me.

"Miss Newman," continued Mr. Seiden, "Have you any objections to my removing Susan Reiner from your homeroom class?"

"But Mr. Seiden," I answered, indignant at the directness of the question, without any introductory preparation for it, "Aren't you going to ask me what happened? Don't you want to hear my side of the episode?"

He squirmed a bit in his chair, and looked at the mother, who was busy smoldering and fidgeting in her seat, across from him.

"You may leave now, Miss Newman. That will be all," he dictated to me, with his gaze averted from me.

I stood there, dumbfounded, at the rudeness of the man, and the unfairness of the manner in which the matter was being handled.

I rushed out of the room, and looked for Bob Arnesen. I saw him in the teachers' workroom, and asked him to walk into a nearby classroom, so we could chat, privately. He agreed, and I told him the whole story about Susan. He listened, intently, and then shook his head, slowly, from side to side, as though he was having difficulty hearing my comments.

"Fran, this is unbelievable. How unfair! You follow Mr. Gordon's orders to check program cards, find a kid with missing signatures on her program card and the kid screams at you, and the next thing you know, Mama writes a letter, and the administration sides with the mother. I'll go and talk with Mr. Seiden the first thing in the morning. If they do this with you, what'll happen to the rest of us? God, it's so unfair. Take it easy, Fran. I'll look for you after lunch tomorrow. I should have spoken to Seiden by then. So long, now. Terry will be wondering where I am."

Bob was moved by the unfairness here and I believe he was sincere in his intention to clear up the matter. So I left the building and went home, too.

Later, the next day, Bob came into the faculty lounge on the second floor, and approached me with a rather strained look on his face.

"Fran," he began slowly, "I spoke to Mr. Seiden about the Reiner girl and he just looked at me, and said, "Bob, the mother was vituperative, so to calm her down, I honored her request."

"My God, Bob, how unfair," I said, amazed at his words. "He gives you that as a reason. Isn't it incredible?"

"I was stunned, Fran. I told him I thought it was very unfair to arbitrarily do whatever a parent asked, just to keep the parent quiet. In this instance, the kid was definitely wrong, and Seiden sells you out and that's that. I told Mr. Seiden that I, as chapter chairman, cannot take this lightly, as a teacher can be undermined and the administration must hear both sides.

I thanked Bob and sat there disheartened and disgusted by this news. I began to realize that no matter what a teacher does, the teacher is wrong, because the administration cares only to please parents, at whatever cost to learning, to standards, to faculty morale. I cringed inwardly, at the futility of trying to get fairness anywhere at Far Rockaway High School.

The days rolled into weeks, and I went about things with my customary enthusiasm but could not really forget the Reiner girl incident. A few days after she was removed by Mr. Gordon from my homeroom, I noticed on the daily absentee sheet that she had also left Far Rockaway High School for Washington Irving, High School.

And then, one day in early March, there was Open School day and Mrs. Feuerstein, mother of Robin Feuerstein, came to see me. I was seated in Room 106, where all the health education teachers were assigned, to meet parents.

She was a woman in her early fifties, serious looking and very direct in her manner towards me. "Miss Newman," she began curtly, "I'm here for one reason and one reason only, and that is to find out why you gave my daughter such a low mark in hygiene this marking period. You do know my Robin, don't you?"

"Yes," I answered, in equally direct fashion, "I know Robin. She's in my hygiene class, and says nothing. She only earned a 65 and that's what I gave her. She sits in the back of the room and does not raise her hand, or try to participate at all. I run a very active class, and encourage my girls to speak out, ask questions, and really take part."

"Well, I never," she exploded. "My Robin is an excellent student, and she's made Arista, the honor society, and you're trying to tell me that she's only worth a 65 in your class, which is after all, a minor.

"I'm sorry you're upset about this, Mrs. Feuerstein," I said to her, firmly, "but when Robin wakes up and begins to actively participate in the class instead of merely occupying a seat, I'm sure she'll do quite well. It's up to her."

"I'll see about this," she sputtered, and stormed out of the room.

She was not unique, in my long experience. Many parents come up and demand a certain mark, and actually try to bribe you into meeting their unfair and unreasonable requests. I've always remained firm, and committed to the idea that the students must do the work, make an honest effort to achieve, and thereby earn whatever grade they receive. School is, after all, a place where the student comes to acquire knowledge and skills which will prepare him/her for the competitive life outside the classroom. Parents who come in to plead and bargain for unearned grades, do their children a disservice, and in my opinion, are cheaters.

When I saw another note from Mr. Gordon in my letterbox, requesting me to come to his office to discuss a parent's complaint, I should not have become upset. I should have been prepared for another one-sided, unprofessional administrative bungling of a simple dispute. But as I read the principal's letter, I felt the tears coming, and decided to ask Bob Arnesen or Abe Gerewitz, our 2 chapter chairmen, to accompany me to this meeting.

Finding Abe, in his science lab, poring over some test papers, I blurted out the whole story, in a kind of non-stop for periods or commas fashion.

Abe listened, nodding his head, and said, in his usual, quiet, sensible way, "Sure, Fran, I'll go in with you. But first let's hear your side of it – what kind of student is Robin – got any test marks to show as examples of how you reached the mark of 65?"

"Yes, Abe, of course, Robin is a blur in the back of the first row. I spend the first couple of weeks in hygiene class, in discussions of first aid, and urge the kids to talk freely, about their own first aid experiences, and they bring in newspaper stories about first aid, and accidents, and we have a very busy scene. Robin just sits there, unresponsive. I've called on her, but she really makes little effort. The students know that I insist on active, class participation; I've explained to them that I get to know them from these class sessions."

"Mrs. Feuerstein is one of these pushy mothers who tries to force a teacher to give high marks so the kids record will look better."

Abe nodded, saying, "Yes, Fran, I know the type. I've met a few myself. Okay, I've got the picture. I'll meet you at the clock at 2:00 and we'll go into Mr. Gordon's office. I agree that you should have a witness, after what Gordon did with the Reiner girl's mother. See you then."

I left the lab feeling relieved, that Abe would come along with me, as I didn't relish facing the principal's icy countenance.

When Abe and I walked in to Mr. Seiden's office, where the meeting was being held, there we saw Mrs. Weidenbaum, Mr. Gordon's other assistant principal, sitting there. Obviously she was going to be Mr. Gordon's witness, and this factor made it all the more comforting to have my own observer there, too.

Immediately upon seeing Abe at my side, Mr. Gordon asked him to leave.

"You have no right to be here, Mr. Gerewitz," he began, "and Miss Newman had no right to ask you to be here, since this is an ordinary, supervisory conference between a principal and a staff member."

"But, Mr. Gordon," Abe replied, quietly, "Miss Newman has a right to be treated fairly, and after the way Mrs. Reiner's complaint was handled, we UFT members feel that teachers here are not being treated equitably, so I, as co-chapter chairman, wish to just listen in. I won't interfere in any way."

Mrs. Weidenbaum sat there, a glare on her sharp-featured face. The principal whitened, and an angry expression appeared on his face.

"I don't see any need for a witness here. This is not a UFT matter. I merely wish to speak to Miss Newman about a parent complaint."

"But you have a witness, Mr. Gordon," I stated, angrily. "Why is Mrs. Weidenbaum here. I've never seen her at a conference before."

The two administrators exchanged glances between them, and suddenly Mr. Gordon said sharply, "All right, let's get on with the meeting but Mr. Gerewitz, you are not to attend this kind of supervisory conference again. Is that clear?"

The threatening overtones apparent in this remark could not be missed here. I caught it and so did Abe. But he didn't say anything. He shrugged his shoulders and stayed put.

"Miss Newman, I have another complaint against you from Mrs. Feuerstein, mother of Robin. Obviously there is something wrong with you, Miss Newman," he began, superciliously, but I interrupted him with, "Why does there automatically have to be something wrong with me! Do you know the whole story, Mr. Gordon, or just what the mother chooses to tell you? She is a very pushy mother and expects to force her will on a teacher." I retorted, annoyed by the approach Mr. Gordon was taking.

"I am sorry, Miss Newman, but there obviously is more here than meets the eye," Mr. Gordon interjected, solemnly.

"Mr. Gordon, I give each student the mark she earns in my classes. Robin is a non-participant in class; she simply sits there, and her quiz marks are low. It's only the first marking period and she can strengthen her efforts and earn as high a mark as she is capable of reaching," I explained.

"You can leave now, Miss Newman," the principal said, flatly. "I've heard enough." "And Mr. Gerewitz, there will be no more of this. When I want to speak to a teacher alone, that is my right, as a supervisor."

Abe just stood there, listening, his face immobile. We walked out together, and chatted briefly, in the corridor.

"Yes, Fran, I see what you mean," Abe began, "There's absolutely no chance with Gordon to receive a fair shake. He will do anything to please a parent. Try to forget this latest incident, and enjoy life outside."

"Yes, sure, Abe, that's what I have always done," I answered, lifelessly, "but I certainly am not enjoying teaching as much as I used to. Do you realize how vulnerable we are, as teachers? Anyone can say anything, at any time, about us, and they'll be believed before the teacher is even consulted. I don't like this, Abe, no not one bit."

He agreed, scratched his head, and pondered a moment, and then excused himself, and we went our separate ways, to find our time cards and leave for the day.

I stopped at the local diner, for a nice, hot cup of coffee, to lift my spirits a bit, and went about life.

A hellish nightmare had begun, but I didn't know this now. How could I know?

Chapter Three

Hearsay Galore:
A Kangaroo Court Hearing

HEARSAY GALORE: A KANGAROO COURT HEARING

On Wednesday, March 19, 1969, Mildred Ashepa, the acting chairman of the Health Education Department, came over to my locker, where I was changing my clothes and blurted, "Swarms of parents are complaining about you. You've lost control." I stood there, shocked by her sudden, serious statement. I answered her by asking who these parents were, and why they were complaining. "I cannot believe anything you say, Mildred," I retorted. "Where are these charges coming from?" She snapped back at me, "Mr. Gordon told me to speak to you about this."

I finished dressing, and ran down the long main hall, to the principal's office, and requested an immediate conference. His secretary, Miss Frant, asked me to wait, as she went into the inner office. About five minutes later, she came out and beckoned me towards the doorway. "Mr. Gordon will see you now, Fran." she said, mechanically.

Mr. Gordon was seated behind his big table, a stern, set expression on his face. "Sit down, Miss Newman," he commanded. "What do you want?" I'll come right to the point, Mr. Gordon. Did you ask Mrs. Ashpa to tell me that swarms of parents are complaining about me?" I asked him. "Indeed, I did, Miss Newman! And what's more, you may as well as know that I'm thinking of sending you to the Board for a medical. You've lost control. You have created many problems." I felt my pulses racing, at this remark, I was becoming angry and demanded. "Mr. Gordon, what have I done? What are you referring to? Who are these swarms of parents you're talking about? What is going on here?"

He looked at me, with his usual supercilious, sneering expression and said, "These parents have complained about you. You need help, Miss Newman." I retorted, "I want to know the names of these parents. Who are they? How can I answer these charges you are

16

making without knowing who these people are? And what do you want to send me to the Board for? I'm a healthy, active, person. I've never felt better in my life. Mr. Gordon, I know all my students and would be very willing to sit down with their parents and discuss any problems or complaints that they may have. But you simply must give me their names." I waited for him to make a reply, but he just sat there, looking at me. I stood up, and began moving towards the door, telling Mr. Gordon that I was going to discuss this matter immediately, with the chapter chairman, Bob Arnesen.

I was upset by the interlude just concluded, and needed to discuss it with someone. Luckily, I located Bob in the teacher's lounge and poured out the events of the past half-hour.

"But he was to give you the names, Fran." Bob said. "How ridiculous! How can you answer a complaint unless you know who made it and what it is? Boy, he's really something! Fran, I'll go down there and speak to him about this. Take it easy! I'll come down to the gym as soon as I talk with him." I was relieved that Bob offered to talk to Mr. Gordon so readily, without my having to ask him.

I taught my next two classes and then went to the women's lounge to do my clerical work, in a quiet place. I needed a few moments to sift through the day's happenings. As this forty minute respite came to an end, I felt more relaxed and began wondering what Bob had learned in the principal's office. I dashed to my locker, changed my clothes and went down to the main office to meet Bob.

Many colleagues were punching the time clock, and after a dozen or so had completed this witless, required chore, along came Bob, his arms laden with exam papers and assorted union publications destined to become stuffing in the faculty letter boxes.

"C'mon, Fran. Help me put these announcements in the boxes and we can talk about what Gordon said, as we do this. Vic said he'd wait for me out front." I grabbed half of the papers and started filling the nearest boxes." What happened, Bob? What did he say to you?" I asked him, eagerly. "Fran, I asked him pointblank what the hell was going on," Bob replied. "And when I mentioned why was he planning to send you to the Board for a medical, he backed off a little. You should have seen him. It was strange." "Bob," I said, puzzled, "I don't exactly know what you mean. Did he deny saying it?" "No,

Fran, he sort of hesitated and said he was only trying to help Miss Newman. He tried to make it seem as though you had blown your mind somehow and he was just trying to be the big, brotherly guy who wants to help you. Boy, it was sickening."

"Bob, did you get the names of the parents? I can't believe that there are any, and it's just his insistence on intimidation. He is such a bully."

"He says he'll hold a meeting during the eighth period on Friday, and you'll get all the names then. "I'll be there, too. It'll be interesting to see what he comes up with. Take it easy, Fran. I gotta run now, as Vic has to take his wife to the doctor now. Bye now." Bob dashed off, and I went on my way, too. I knew now, that I was going to get the names of the parents who were complaining about me, and felt confident that the whole matter would be cleared up on Friday.

Friday, March 21, 1969, started off uneventfully, but oh, my God, it was a fateful day in many ways. It changed me from a trusting, believing, respecter of authority, into a much more aware and realistic and determined person. As events unfolded right in front of my eyes, and I saw and heard things from the most unexpected sources and for previously unknown motivations, I was forced by circumstance to become totally aware of everything happening around me, every day, every minute.

It was necessary for me to keep my eyes and ears wide open, as a detective in an Agatha Christie story might, in order to survive the hostile climate in which I was living each day.

While emptying my letterbox, I met Allie Metzger, a male gym teacher in my department whom I liked a respected as a person and as a teacher. He had just recently passed the license examination to become a department chairman, and I was very happy for him, as he was an earnest, sincere guy with a friendly manner and a wry wit. Seeing him there in the lounge that Friday, I spontaneously invited him to sit in on the meeting the principal was holding, saying, "Allie, since you're going to be a department chairman pretty soon, you might find attending this meeting a valuable experience. I'm trying to find out who the complaining parents are. It should be an interesting meeting. Will you come?"

"Sure, Fran, I'll be there. Thanks for letting me know. See you later," he said, grinning at me.

Somehow, my classes were taught, my lunch was eaten, and my desire to get to the bottom of Mr. Gordon's threats was sufficiently subdued for me to do a normal day's work and then, here it was, period 8, Friday, March 21, 1969. I entered Mr. Gordon's office and found Bob Arnesen standing in the anteroom, waiting for me.

"Hi, Fran, hope you're okay. Just be calm and listen," he said quietly. "I'll take notes and am sure this whole thing can be cleared today." I'm not so sure, Bob," I answered. "Let's go in. I'm ready."

We were directed to our seats at the far end of the table by Mr. Gordon. I saw administrators' faces everywhere. Mrs. Weidenbaum, a sharp-faced woman, who arrived at Far Rockaway High School with Mr. Gordon and became one of his assistant principals, was seated to my right, next to Mr. Seiden, the other assistant principal. My acting chairman, Mrs. Ashepa, was next – then came Allie Metzger, who was there at my request.

At least, I thought so, at the time.

Even seeing his name on Mr. Gordon's memo about this meeting hadn't made me think otherwise.

Alice Nirenberg, also a member of my department, was at the table, and at the far end, to my left, was Lester Marks, the newly arrived school psychologist. I wondered what he was doing here as he had just become a member of the staff, perhaps six weeks ago, as part of a new program called Operation Aspiration Search.

Mr. Gordon coughed and began the meeting. "Ladies and gentlemen, we're gathered here today to help Miss Newman. She has lost control and has created serious problems in the school by her inability to handle parents and students." "I object to your remarks, Mr. Gordon," I interjected. "I asked you to give me the names of the students, when you've been here just over a month and are testifying against a teacher who has been here fifteen years. Did you ever consult me about these so-called complaints?" "Did you try to find out why these students were griping? Has the thought occurred to you that their complaints may be totally unjustified?"

"Miss Newman, we've heard enough from you," barked Mr. Gordon. "Please raise your hand when you want to speak; don't just start shouting."

"I am not shouting, Mr. Gordon," I lashed back. "You saw that I wished to speak but did not give me the courtesy of the opportunity."

"We will continue now." the principal said. "Let's hear from you next, Mr. Seiden." This obese man had always been friendly to me. I could not imagine what he would say.

"This teacher has been seen eating lunch alone in the cafeteria since the strike. I believe this is a sign of mental strain!"

Bob turned to me, shook his head, and shrugged. I stood up and objected strenuously to this statement. "Mr. Seiden, how dare you make such a ridiculous remark." Since when is my choice of luncheon partners an administrative concern? And because I've lost respect for many of my colleagues who would not participate in the strike, I preferred reading the New York Times. You're accusing me of suffering mental strain. Baloney! I have self-respect and do not wish to associate with those who are first on the new benefits line when I do all the work to help get these improvements." "It's frankly none of your business whom I eat lunch with, Mr. Seiden. I am amazed that you could be so petty."

Mr. Gordon glared at me and said, "Have you finished, Miss Newman?" I don't appreciate your outbursts and ask you again to please control yourself, so we may continue."

"Mr. Gordon," I answered back, "Where are the names of the complaining parents? This was the purpose of the meeting, not a character assassination. Right, Mr. Arnesen?"

Bob looked up at the assembled group, from his note-taking, a puzzled look on his face, and shook his head, looking very concerned.

"Mr. Gordon," he said, "I agree with Fran. You haven't brought up a single name of a complainant. Let's get to some real people, please, if there are any."

"Mr. Arnesen," the principal said harshly, "Kindly confine your remarks to what is being said here, not your opinion on what is being said. There's a difference, you know."

Bob looked nonplussed and lowered his gaze to that convenient note pad. "I'll ask you for your comments now, Mrs. Ashepa, and then you'll have your turn, Mr. Metzger."

Mr. Metzger? I couldn't believe what I had just heard. So Mr. Metzger had come here to testify against me. And he knew this earlier in the day and had not cared to tell me, allowing me to think he would be here because I had invited his attendance. I was frankly hurt, but kept my face without expression. No matter what he was going to say, it was such a despicable act on his part.

"Mr. Gordon, I'd like to add that Miss Newman spent a lot of her class time collecting money for all the school fund drives, when she should have been teaching." Mildred Ashepa said, deliberately, with malice hanging onto every syllable. A firm, set expression accompanied this utterance of hers. Everyone looked at her, and I jumped up and said, "That's a deliberate exaggeration of my efforts," "When Mr. Seiden asked me to collect for the various charity drives, I was only too happy to help him. I trained a lot of my students to count the money and hand out receipts while they worked for me in the gym. They never interfered with my teaching my classes, so Mrs. Ashepa is lying." "I resent her remarks, and Mr. Gordon, I wish to go on record as saying that this so-called meeting seems like a gang-rape attack, or a Kangaroo Court where the victim hasn't a remote chance."

"Yes, that is true, and as the U.F.T. chapter chairman for this faculty, I agree with Miss Newman," Bob Arnesen said. "From what I've heard here so far, Mr. Gordon, I feel you are all giving your opinions about Fran's activities and personality. We're supposed to be learning what the actual complaints are and thus far the meeting is a farce."

"Mr. Arnesen," Mr. Gordon said in a strong voice, "Miss Newman's behavior and handling of parents and students has created serious problems at this school, and I'm doing my duty as principal here to correct the situation."

"Mr. Gordon, you are confused here. I asked you on Wednesday afternoon to give me the names of the complainants. You said 'there were swarms of names'. I'm asking now, that you reveal this information so Fran can defend herself."

"I do not need your help in organizing a meeting, Mr. Arnesen. I am the principal and I decide what's done and where and by whom, is that clear? I also want to add that Miss Newman's intensity concerning the strike was abnormal, in my opinion."

"I beg your pardon, Mr. Gordon, but your opinion is uncalled for here," I said, "The total apathy of most of our staff during those bitter weeks of the strike would make anyone who actively participated seem militant. I was no more active than Mr. Arnesen and a few others, yet you have not called them abnormal."

"You are labeling Miss Newman," Mr. Arnesen said, "And if this continues, I shall advise Miss Newman to file a Step One Grievance immediately."

Mr. Gordon then peered at his assistant principals as though expecting them to comment but they said nothing. Only their expressions denoted interest in the proceedings.

"Please tell us your facts here, Mr. Metzger. Sorry to have kept you waiting so long, but with Miss Newman interrupting every minute, with her outbursts, things have gotten delayed. And Miss Nirenberg, you can present your charges, here, as soon as Mr. Metzger completes his statements."

Miss Nirenberg, a dark haired, self-effacing type of person, whose fluttery gestures constantly belied her insecurity, smiled and said nothing.

"All I have to add here," began Allie Metzger, hesitantly, "is what I told you in your office, Mr. Gordon."

"Just tell it here, please," the principal said. "It is very significant."

"Well, at the beginning of this term, about 5 or 6 girls came into my office and asked to have their programs changed, saying they had Miss Newman for gym and didn't want to be in her class. I told them I wouldn't change their classes for such flimsy reason."

"What students," I demanded, "Name them, Mr. Metzger."

"I didn't bother to ask their names," he retorted. "Lots of kids ask for program changes because they heard something about a teacher from a friend or someone was failed by a teacher and they're afraid the same fate awaits them. I don't encourage shopping around for teachers."

"Allie," said Bob Arnesen, "You came here to tell this nonsense as a charge against Miss Newman – anonymous people making unkind comments about a teacher they've never had. Mr. Gordon, I'd like to leave now. This meeting is vicious and nothing but a Kangaroo Court. I can't believe what I've seen and heard today."

"Bob, Mr. Gordon has asked me to be here today, and I came to do what he asked," replied Allie, whose face seemed to be quivering.

I did not honor those girls' requests so nothing really has happened to Fran, because of me, right, Bob?"

"I'll answer that," I lashed out. "Your willingness to be here is really the whole issue. If some of my students complained about me, why didn't you speak to me about it? Why go behind my back to Mr. Gordon?"

"Yes, Allie, you're surely not a friend. Fran has always spoken so highly of you. I admit I'm surprised to see you here today," Bob said, tartly.

"Mr. Metzger, thank you for your comments," the principal bellowed. "Miss Nirenberg, let's hear from you now. Please be specific as the period is almost over."

"Well, Miss Newman insulted a Puerto Rican mother last Open School nite. She mimicked her, and then a few minutes later, she insulted another mother. It was awful," the dean said, hesitantly.

"Who are you referring to, Alice? What are the names of the parents? I demand to know, right now. I'm fed up with all this hearsay," I spoke out sharply. "Mr. Gordon, this meeting has been an insult from start to finish. I'm filing a Step One immediately, Mr. Gordon. Please come with me, Bob. I want to leave this meeting now."

"Yes, Fran, let's go," Bob agreed. "Mr. Gordon, I'll place the Step One grievance appear in your letterbox first thing in the morning."

As we started towards the door, I couldn't resist a last remark to this assemblage. "Mr. Gordon, and the rest of you who came here, I want to reiterate how despicable this all is – if you have a complaint, spell it out. I know Miss Nirenberg meant the parents of Nilsa Figueroa and Ellen Buchanan; these mothers came to Open School nite yelling and lying and in general acting as though their daughters were ideal students. Both of these girls have big files in the dean's office as cutters and behavior problems and Ellen has a heavy dossier of difficulty all the way back to junior high school. Why are you bringing up what I said to them five months ago? If I erred, why wait to correct the mistake? Mr. Gordon, I will not be intimidated by you or anyone else."

fMy torrent of protest fell on everyone's ears. As the bell rang, ending the period, all these lackeys of the principal ran away, like rats scurrying back to their holes when a cat comes near.

Outside the room, shaking with disgust, I turned to Bob and said, "Oh, Bob, how awful, not one parent's name was revealed. They only want to intimidate and humiliate me. I resent it. I will fight this."

"Yes, Fran, you should. I'll file Step One tomorrow. Meanwhile, call the U.F.T. and let them know we are filing. Try 'n' take it easy," he said, in a reassuring tone. "See you tomorrow."

At U.F.T., Ed Kochian listened to my story, and then began yelling at me. "What's so terrible, Miss Newman? So your principal tried to intimidate you and threatened to send you to the board for a medical! The fact is that he hasn't put anything in writing, or in your file, right?"

"Yes, but I don't want him to get away with his claims of parental complaints and holding a Kangaroo Court with supervisors insulting me." "Please do something!" A feeling of urgency rose up within me.

"Listen, honey," he went on, in a very unsympathetic tone, "You can go ahead and file a Step One if it'll make you feel better. But we only deal with complaints in writing. We can't go after a principal who just verbally threatens a teacher. It'll be his word against ours and will end up a waste of our time. Try not to make a big deal out of it, Okay?"

"Mr. Kochian, your attitude certainly surprises me. You're not very friendly, I'd say," I answered him.

"Miss Newman, we try to do what we can, but we don't have enough time or enough manpower to handle every minor complaint. You've gotta try to understand."

"I only understand that an awful thing was done to me today. I'm absolutely shaken up by it. I'm filing a Step One grievance and since there's not a glimmer of hope that I'd win, with Mr. Gordon as the hearing officer, I'm letting you know in advance, that I want to file a Step Two grievance to the district superintendent." I retorted, angry at his indifference.

"Okay, Miss Newman, have it your way," he said, in a cajoling tone." Have your chapter chairman call me to keep me informed – good luck!" He hung up, and I slammed the receiver down very hard.

In a few days, the Step One hearing was held. Bob and I discussed what we'd say, at lunch.

"Fran, just remain calm. I'll do the talking," Bob began firmly. "I'll ask again for the names of the complaining parents. If the question is evaded, I'll tell Mr. Gordon that we'll take the matter up with the Superintendent Schwab at Step Two, okay?"

"Yes, Bob, that's good. Brevity and specificity will either do it or show him up once and for all," I replied.

At the hearing is Mr. Gordon's office, I felt we were dealing with a concrete wall. Mr. Gordon insisted that he had had swarms of complaints against me, but still refused to identify complainants by name, just innuendo. When Bob insisted that we know, Mr. Gordon simply tightened up and attacked me again, saying he had to do something to protect the students from this "terrible teacher" – me – "who had done such terrible things." When 'swarms' of parents whom you say have complained about me." "I didn't ask you for your opinions about me. Isn't that correct, Mr. Arnesen?"

"Yes, this is correct, Mr. Gordon," Bob replied, hastily. "You charged Miss Newman with being the teacher whom many parents are complaining about. This meeting is a direct outcome of her request, and my seconding of it, so that Miss Newman may explain her side of the situation. I'd like to help in any way I can, in my role as chairman. May we please move ahead, therefore?"

The principal did not acknowledge our statements and continued, tersely. "All of you have knowledge of her difficulties. Mr. Marks, will you please begin now?"

The psychologist stood up and said in an authoritative manner, "I have heard some terrible things about this teacher from the students," and sat down, stiffly.

I couldn't believe my ears. I never had had any contact with this man. I turned to Bob and whispered, "How dare he testify against me like that?"

Bob agreed, saying, "I'll ask him which students." "Mr. Marks," he queried, "Which students are you referring to?"

"Yes, Mr. Marks," I added sarcastically, "I'd like to know who complained about me, and to add that I think you have some nerve. Bob asked what I had done, the principal evaded the question, but only to stress again how awful what I had done was, and how many administrative problems my actions had created for him, this sensitive, caring man, who only wanted to "protect these innocent, harassed students from this out-of-control gym teacher."

Bob and I both felt frustrated, and hopeless, and left Mr. Gordon's office in an angry mood at having completely wasted our time. The Step One level is a sham –a farce, and cannot possibly be fair to any grievant.

As we were leaving, Mr. Gordon suggested to Bob and me that we go directly to Mr. Marks, the psychologist, and to Mrs. Ashepa, the acting head of my department and to Miss Nirenberg, the dean of girls, for the actual names of the complaining parents.

Bob recanted the fact that this information was to have been revealed at the March 21, 1969 meeting, so that I could answer the charges. He also said that the group Mr. Gordon now suggested we go to see, were present at that March meeting and they did not mention a single name.

Mr. Gordon looked at Bob, menacingly, and hissed, "They have all the names. They brought them to me."

We walked out of the office!

Outside, Bob said, "Listen, Fran, he's impossible!" He added warmly, "He's trying to make it seem as though Marks and Ashepa and Nirenberg came to him, about you, when you and I know it was the reverse."

"You bet, Bob," I agreed. "Gordon is trying to intimidate me, simply because I refuse to be scared by him. When are we going to talk to these three?"

"I'm free tomorrow per 8," he replied, "and so are you, right, Fran?" "I'd like Tom Dente to interview Marks, too. Since Tom is a grade adviser, I think he should hear what the new school psychologist said about you, and why. What do you think?"

"Good idea, Tom would be a big help, I think," I responded. I'm going home now, Bob, I'm thoroughly exhausted. Thanks for your help today."

On the way home, my memory bank spun out the events of the day and by the time I reached my apartment, a feeling of despair and helplessness had enveloped me.

As the fifth period bell rang, next day, I went to Tom Dente's office and met Bob there.

"Hi, Fran. Glad you're here early." said Tom. "Lester Marks is coming right in. Right after we speak with him, we'll go to Alice's office and get her names, also," Bob said, jotting notes on the pad he usually carried.

"Good, Bob," I replied. "Let's get it over with as soon as possible. I'm so curious. The more I ponder about it, the more I can't think of who the parents might be."

"From what I gather, Fran," Tom added, "the meeting was a farce, right? So don't get your hopes too high."

"I won't, Tom. But I have a right to know who's accusing me of what." I countered.

"Yes, of course," Tom said, "But I really can't understand how this guy Marks got in on this in the first place. Hell, he's only been here a few weeks. Oh, there he is now. Over here, Mr. Marks, please." "Sit down at the table," Bob directed. "We'll be brief. Please tell us how you came to testify against Miss Newman when you have never spoken to her or consulted with her, at all." "You don't even know, Fran," added Tom sharply. "It's a pretty low way to behave, I think."

This short, stocky, bearded man, answered Tom, while glaring at me." "I heard some terrible things from the kids and I said so."

"But who are these kids, Mr. Marks? And why didn't you come to Fran, to discuss what these complaints were?" asked Bob.

"She's a snob," Lester Marks lashed back. "I see her walking down the hall with her nose in the air, as if she owns the place."

"I'm not interested in your opinions of Fran," Bob said, with urgency in his voice. "We're here to get the names of the kids. Let's have them, Mr. Marks, now, please."

"Oh no, I'm not giving you any names," this nasty psychologist answered, harshly." "You'll have to go to Mr. Gordon for those. I'm not telling you anything."

Tom Dente was listening intently, and then posed this question to Mr. Marks. "How do you see your role here, at the school, Mr.

27

Marks? Are you going to run into the principal's office with complaints from the kids without checking with the teachers? You do realize, don't you, that lots of kids lie and exaggerate in order to protect themselves? Isn't it only fair to hear the teacher's side of a problem?"

"I'm only doing my job," he replied testily. "I will perform my role as school psychologist any way I please."

"In that case," countered Tom, his voice steady and calm, "I'll hold a meeting of the grade advisors and tell them what you've just said and you may find that no students will be referred to you, by anyone."

"Good idea, Tom," Bob chimed in. "I'll tell the whole staff at the next U.F.T. meeting that the new school psychologist goes directly to Mr. Gordon and doesn't check out stories told by the kids. He assumes the teacher is guilty!"

Mr. Marks squirmed in his chair but said nothing.

I had been listening and observing, and decided to speak up. "I've been teaching here for 16 years, and you have been here about 6 weeks and are judging me, on hearsay and rumor, you scared little bastard." I said, looking directly at him. "You feel insecure, so anyone who looks and is self-assured and comfortable becomes a threat to you. So a good way to hurt this person is to be a witness at a Kangaroo court. How despicable!"

"I have nothing personal against you, Miss Newman," he hissed back. "I was only doing my job."

Bob and Tom stood up, and began leaving Tom's office.

"C'mon, Fran. Let's go to the dean before the period's over." suggested Bob. "I think we've got the picture here."

The three of us left abruptly, not even bothering to say anything further. Lester Marks was sitting there, woodenly, as we left.

Alice Nirenberg, the gym teacher-turned dean, was alone in her office as we entered. She looked up, puzzled, as Bob and I came towards her.

"What brings you here, Bob?" she queried, ignoring my presence. "Please sit down!" Alice pointed to two chairs, and we sat down.

"Mr. Gordon sent us to you, Alice, for the names of the parents and students who've been complaining about Fran," Bob began, "He says you gave him names."

Alice reddened, dropped a pencil, picked it up, and said shrilly, glaring at me. "Get her out of here. She's bothering me!"

"What are you screaming about Alice?" Bob asked her. "Fran isn't bothering you. You made some charges against her at that sickening meeting and I'm here to get all the names, so Fran can answer the complaints. You were Fran's friend. How could you do this to her?"

Alice Nirenberg glowered and shook, and pointed her finger towards the door. "Bob," she sputtered, anger etched into her expression, "please get out of here, now. I don't have to tell her or you anything! If you want names, go to Mr. Gordon. Leave me alone!"

She slammed her door as we departed.

"My God, what phonies," I said to Bob. "It's absolutely disgusting."

"Fran, Alice and this guy Marks were not only rude, but reveal themselves to be totally rotten individuals. I figure that Gordon told them not to divulge any information when we come to them, thereby making it seem as though he's re-operating, get it?" Bob elucidated, as we walked back to Fran's office.

"Yes, I get it. Bob." I answered, moodily. "I'm so disgusted. We're going in circles. Ashepa will probably pull the same stunt."

"No doubt about it, Fran." he agreed. "But we'll see her period 8 and then we will call the Union office for further instructions. You'll want to file for a Step Two hearing right away!"

"You bet I'll file, Bob," I shot back at him." "Maybe the district superintendent, or, what's her name, Schwab, will realize that we live in America and no one can answer charges made by invisible sources. Honestly, Bob, isn't this incredible?"

"Yes, Fran. It's hard for me to understand, too. Take it easy. Keep calm," he responded, wearily. Meet me at the clock, period 8, and we'll go to your chairman together. I'm giving a quiz this period and have to go upstairs now. So long." He dashed up the stairs and I headed for the cafeteria.

My next two classes ran smoothly and period 8 was now here, and there was Bob, at the clock, chatting with several teachers. We all exchanged a few words, and Bob separated himself from them, motioned me towards the door.

When we reached the door of the health education office, Bob said, "I'll ask her for the names, Fran. Try to just listen and let me do the talking. It'll be better, I think," he said seriously.

I nodded, as he knocked, and we entered the office.

"Mildred, we're here to get some names of complaining parents. Mr. Gordon told us you were the source of some of the complaints." Bob began, in a business like tone. Mildred snarled at him as she answered, "I'm not giving you any names. I don't have to talk to you at all."

Bob's expression denoted disgust. It matched mine, I'm sure.

"Gordon said you would give us the names so obviously you went to him with complaints. Please don't waste our time. Give Fran and me the names of all the people, now." he requested, in a very forceful tone.

'I'll give you nothing, Bob." she stated, in an acid tone. "Now please get out of here, I'm busy. She lowered her gaze and we got up and left the office.

"She's really something, Fran. What a crummy attitude!" Bob said sympathetically.

"It's outrageous, Bob." I answered. "Please call Mr. Kochian and tell him we want to file a Step Two, the minute we get Gordon's decision on Step One. I can't stand this. It has shades of the Gestapo boys." I was on the verge of tears. The frustration was overwhelming.

"Take it easy, Fran." Bob said, trying to sooth me. "I'm going to take care of everything. I'll call Abe tonight, too. This was really a dirty deal. I've never known anything else like it, to tell you the truth."

"I'm meeting some friends for dinner tonight, Bob." I told him. "Wait till I tell them, they won't believe it."

"Good, have a nice evening, Fran. Don't let this get you down." he said. "I'll get in touch with you, the minute Gordon writes his Step One decision.

We parted, each to go his own way.

At dinner, I told my friends, also teachers, of the events that transpired that day. They looked aghast. Both were upset and tried to soothe me. Somehow, they both felt the matter would be solved at

Step Two. They couldn't conceive of the district superintendent being anything but anxious to resolve this difficult matter. But I couldn't feel as confident as they. I promised to keep my friends posted on developments as we said goodnight.

Several days later, Mr. Gordon's denial of my grievance appeared in the letterbox. Naturally, he being both the judge and the accused, the outcome was predictable. Step One had become a complete farce, a sham.

In his denial, Mr. Gordon insisted that he had every right to threaten me, to not tell me the names of the complaining parents, and it was obvious that my insistence on knowing infuriated him as his vehemence could not be overlooked. One simply could not expect a shred of decency from him.

The intervening days, while awaiting the Step Two appeal hearing were filled with routine tasks, and mounting tension.

Bob Arnesen and Abe Gerewitz and I conferred about the hearing and a U.F.T. grievance representative, Allen Griggs, had been assigned to assist us at the hearing, too. His role was to present my side, and help Bob Arnesen in the interplay that would take place. The Union's representatives at these hearings would, therefore, in a sense, have an expert to counsel him on how to proceed.

Bob and I arrived at Public School 66, in Richmond Hill, where District Superintendent Rose Schwab maintained her office, about 15 minutes early. We conferred with Mr. Griggs as to how things should go.

Superintendent Schwab, a colorless, middle-aged, rather pompous woman was in the small office as we entered. She looked stoney-faced. The male stenotypist was already seated there, as was Mr. Gordon. We three sat down to what turned out to be one of the most outrageous meetings I would be attending in the next two years.

Bob Arnesen stated my reasons for requesting this hearing. Superintendent Schwab leaned on her fleshy elbows, and turning toward me, asked, "What have you to say, Miss Newman?"

"Superintendent Schwab, Mr. Gordon has threatened me with the charge that swarms of parents have been complaining about me," I began, firm voiced. "When I asked him————,"

"Lower your voice, Miss Newman. Stop yelling." interrupted Mrs. Schwab, in a most rude manner.

I looked at her, temporarily speechless, at this gross behavior. Somehow, I did not expect it, from a woman in such a high position. I turned toward Bob Arnesen and Allan Griggs, hoping they would object to the tone of the Superintendent's comment, but although they appeared surprised, they said nothing.

"If I may continue now," I said, very quietly, "I asked Mr. Gordon for the names of the complaining parents, so that I could tell my side. I offered to bring in my records, and sit down with these parents and discuss their problems."

"Yes, Mrs. Schwab," Bob Arnesen added, "We never were able to obtain the parents names from Mr. Gordon even after many attempts. He seems to indulge in hearsay and innuendo. It's impossible for Miss Newman to answer charges made by invisible people."

"Is that all?" queried Mrs. Schwab, an intent, yet totally non-committal expression on her face.

"No," I hastily interjected, "Mr. Gordon held a so-called meeting at which he promised to reveal the parents names. Instead, it turned out to be an administrative kangaroo court. It was a degrading experience and I filed a Step One grievance, which was, of course, denied by Mr. Gordon, and, "————————

"That's enough, Miss Newman," the Superintendent said, sharply, "I'd like to go now." Her abrupt manner was upsetting me, as it evinced a certain "uncaring, let's get this petty annoyance over quickly" attitude, and hardly radiated impartiality.

"Let's have the names of these complaining parents, please, Mr. Gordon," Mrs. Schwab asked, in a soft voice. "I'd like to hear what their dissatisfactions are."

"Superintendent Schwab," began Mr. Gordon, in a low, level tone. "Here is a folder I have prepared for you." He placed a manila folder on the table, in front of her. Mrs. Schwab opened it, glanced at the top page, and closed the folder, quickly.

"Thank you, Mr. Gordon, I shall read it carefully after the meeting," she cooed. "Let's get on with it."

With arms folded across his chest, and an expression of disdain etched into his sharp features, the principal issued the following statement.

"Superintendent Schwab, the parents who have complained have asked to remain anonymous. They are afraid this teacher will be vindictive."

I was aghast. Allen Grigg's face on my immediate left, registered surprise, as did Bob Arnesen's, on my right.

We waited with baited breath, for Superintendent Schwab's answer to Mr. Gordon's statement.

She looked at Mr. Gordon, at her nails, shifted her ample form around in her chair and said, "Well, Miss Newman, although you may not like it, that's the way it is. I'll adjourn this meeting now and make my decision within the next ten days.

I tried to object. I stood up and sputtered about this being the United States, 1969, not Soviet Russia, or Nazi Germany, and a person cannot defend herself against anonymous, invisible swarms.

Allen Griggs and Bob Arnesen made a weak attempt, also, to voice their opinions, but Superintendent Schwab's voice, and manner, as she stood up to smile at Mr. Gordon, and her male assistant, who took the minutes, left no room for any further action. The hearing was over.

Tears of frustration poured from me as we left. Shock, disbelief and disgust were the feelings that surged through me. My two defenders tried to reassure me and calm me, but I could see, even now, the futility of getting a shred of fair treatment from a Board of Education administrator.

I asked Mr. Griggs to start readying a Step three appeal right away, since there seemed to be no doubt as to the decision Mrs. Schwab would write.

Chapter Four

The Gym Teacher Wore Pantyhose

THE GYM TEACHER WORE PANTYHOSE

My gym class began streaming in from the locker room stairway and some of the girls were already seating themselves on their assigned floor spots. The two assisting teachers were already doing their assigned tasks, checking notes and interviewing returning absentees, as well as helping the girls to assemble in an orderly and safe manner. It was time for me to blow my whistle and call the class to attention. Walking to the front of the gymnasium, I placed myself in a back-to-wall position, facing the students. They quieted down, gradually, and waited for me to announce the lesson plan we would follow this morning.

One hundred forty-five seniors and juniors sat there, with that familiar look of expectancy that after more than twenty years of teaching health education, I have come to recognize as a plea for mercy and as light a burden of physical exertion as possible. The look was a nonverbal way of asking me not to ask them to exercise strenuously, because intricate hairdos would come unfastened and perspiration would smear all that carefully applied mascara and heaven forbid we might achieve that worthy goal that I had set for them, namely physical fitness!

I started to explain that since we were working on a modern dance unit now, I would like them to do a leg stretch about eight times, since it was an excellent limbering movement. Directing the class to assume a comfortable, spread-eagle position, with their legs placed as far apart as possible, and arms raised over-head, I waited a few seconds, before continuing, thus allowing a little time for the groans and screeches of protest at this "difficult" assignment.

"Practice while I get on the platform, girls," I said "I'll do this stretch with you." They buzzed a bit and waited for me to get into position. "Ready," I called out to them "Start your stretch to the right side and then we'll alternate from right to left, to a steady, slow count of one, two, three, four."

As I leaned forward to sweep my left arm across my right knee, I noticed the tear in the crotch of my pantyhose. Taken aback momentarily, I quickly placed my hand over the torn seam and pulled my skirt forward to cover the whole area. Trying to diminish the impact of this occurrence, I said to the class, "Oh, my goodness, I'm popping my seams. Guess I'll just have to cut out those delicious Danish at breakfast." At the same time, I urged them to finish along with me for another few counts. I then stood up on the platform, preparing to go on with the lesson.

They were tittering, and poking each other, and making comments about what had happened. Their noisy reaction was quite natural under the circumstances. After all, a very private area of their teacher's anatomy was suddenly highlighted, in an unexpected way. Surely you and I would have reacted similarly.

I had to be quite firm with the students now, as I tried to get them into their twelve dance groups. They were a little unruly, and it took at least three or four minutes of stern and repetitive commands to get them ready to do their across-the-floor movements. Finally, they were under control and leaped and skipped and pranced to my cues until it was time for dismissal.

"See you tomorrow, girls" I said. "Please dress quickly and get down here early, so you can practice these patterns we tried today. O.K., you may leave now," I said, feeling a sense of relief. Putting away a few volley balls that were lying on the floor, I also tidied up the gym desk a bit and picked up my marking folders. The passing bell rang and it was time to go to my next assignment.

The next day will remain in my memory for a lifetime.

I taught the same class the next day, and all went smoothly and routinely. Not a single student said anything to me about the previous day's incident and neither did the two assisting teachers. These young substitutes and I had very little to do with each other, except on a strictly professional level. I had had enough contact with both of them before this term, in the gym and in the health education office, to decide that they were not the kind of people I would seek to cultivate as friends. The three of us had our duties to perform in the gym, and as long as they were done, things went along neatly enough.

In the last period of the day, I was working in the girls' emergency room, checking and filling medical notes that students had brought in. No one was with me; it was very peaceful.

I knew that there was a male teacher on duty next door, in the boys' emergency room, because two teachers were assigned there all through the day. The door between the two rooms was open, and I could hear someone dialing a number on the phone on the wall near the window.

Suddenly my acting chairman, Mrs. Ashepa, was standing there, peering over my shoulder. I was absorbed in the details of a medial excuse note, and hadn't heard her come up behind me. She said in a very controlled voice, "You are the laughing stock of the school. I want you to wear underpants. And I want you to stop wearing street shoes in the gym, instead of sneakers. This is department policy."

Taken by surprise at her nasty words, I stepped back and retorted, "What the hell are you talking about?"

She fumed back, "It was reported to me that your pantyhose ripped yesterday and your pubic hairs were showing and all the students were embarrassed and very upset by your performance. You are sick, sick, sick!"

Having completed her insulting tirade, she stood there, staring at me in a condescending manner. I looked at her squarely, and answered her in kind. "Who do you think you're talking to, you bitch? Who do you think you are? I'm going to file a grievance against you right now, and put a stop to you!"

I rushed out through the boys' emergency room, to look for Bob Arnesen, the United Federation of Teachers chapter chairman. I knew he could be found in Room 202, directly overhead. But right there, Mr. Kobren, the assigned teacher that period, sat and looked at me, quizzically. However, he didn't follow up with a comment, which seemed frozen into his expression.

I was certain that he had overheard the exchange between Mrs. Ashepa and me, and suddenly I wanted to hear him say so; it seemed very important that there be a witness. I questioned him, in a pleading way. "Sidney, did you hear her? Did you hear those insults? What's so terrible about these pantyhose, hmm?" I was seething with anger now, and in a kind of gesture of ventilation, I flicked my skirt across my knees and lifted I above them, slightly.

His reply was so unexpected that I just stood there, unable to move. "You've got great legs, Fran. But I don't want to get involved. I didn't hear anything."

Mrs. Ashepa was standing by in the doorway, too. I hadn't noticed her until now. Her supercilious smile gave me impetus, and I left the room.

Finding Bob upstairs, seated at the big worktable, marking history test, I blurted out all the details in a non-stop torrent. I was on the verge of tears by now, too. He listened, attentively, and said, "What's she making such a big fuss about? Anyone could have an accident like that. And calling you sick, too. That's an insult if I ever heard one. Yes, Fran, I agree with you. This is harassment again. I'll go right down and talk to her about this. Please join me in the health education office as soon as you get U.F.T. headquarters on the phone."

I agreed to meet him as soon as I filed the grievance with the main office and left the room. I made the call to the grievance office, and was advised to come right down after school to begin processing the complaint. I was calmer now; I felt supported, and knew that soon I would get some relief.

I walked back to the health education office to meet Bob and to see if he was making any headway with the chairman. I could hear Mrs. Ashepa declaring that "She's sick, and a terrible person. I'm going to do something about her."

As I opened the door, Bob was trying to reason with her, saying that anyone's pants could tear. "It could happen to anyone." he said, vehemently. "It was an accident, a momentary thing, and should be forgotten."

She continued to insist that the assisting teachers had come to her, telling her that they were very embarrassed by the incident and very upset by the way I chose to handle it.

Bob retorted that she was making a minor occurrence into a "big deal," and said he hoped that if his wife ever had a similar accident, her supervisor would be more understanding and would not make such an issue of the matter.

Mrs. Ashepa glowered at him and bellowed back with the allegation that all the students in my class had come in to complain about me and that she, as acting chairman, was going to have to do something about it.

"Bob," I asked, "What right does she have to call me sick?

Ask her to name a kid who came in to complain. I'm sure that none of them came in at all. Mrs. Ashepa has a tendency to exaggerate everything."

Bob looked at her, very directly, and said firmly, "You have no right to talk to Fran or any teacher this way and I'm going down to the principal's office right now to see if we can clear this matter up. C'mon, Fran. Get your coat and I'll walk down the hall with you."

As we made our way down the long corridor to the main teachers' workroom and through the cluster of secretarial offices, he attempted to soothe me and said he' do everything he could to get the principal to act in the matter. Neither of us expected fair play or impartiality from Mr. Gordon, however. Somehow, things always worked out in favor of the people against whom I was making the complaint.

I said goodbye to Bob, punched my timecard, and left the school. The fresh air felt good as I stepped outside the building. Digging deep into my purse for my car keys, I found them at first grab. I opened my car door and tumbled in. A feeling of frustration clamped its way through my whole body, but knowing I had a twenty-five mile drive ahead of me, I forced myself to concentrate on driving carefully.

An hour and ten minutes later, I was parking in front of U.F.T. headquarters at Park Avenue South and Twenty-first Street. The elevator was there and I stepped in, eagerly. The second floor grievance department was my destination. I knew Mr. Speranza, the chief grievance officer, would be waiting for me since I had worked with him before, and found him to be a very sincere and empathetic man, well-suited to the work he was doing.

"Hello, there, Fran," he said cheerfully. "Pull up a chair and tell me the whole story again. Want some coffee, huh?"

I poured out my grievance, from the incident itself, to the scene in my office an hour and a half earlier. He made a few notes on a pad, but said nothing until I had finished. Then he gave me his opinion on how to proceed. "Fran, it's harassment again. There's no question in my mind that she's out to get you because you objected last January to her being asked to fill in as chairman while Mr. Rommer was on leave. This is just the opportunity she was looking for to get you.

The whole thing is ridiculous. You and I both know that, but proving it is something else again. Let's be realistic."

I nodded in agreement as he continued.

"If Bob succeeds in getting a preliminary meeting with Gordon, maybe it won't be necessary to file a formal grievance. But I doubt that you'll get any satisfaction there, so go ahead and file a grievance, by all means. Tell Bob to keep me posted on what happens. And Fran, try to realize that it's going to be tough on you in that school. Take it easy. Don't let it get you down. There are a lot of nasty, insecure people around. Good luck!"

I left feeling a lot better. At least Mr. Speranza knew what had happened. He had heard my side of the story directly from me, rather than from some third of fourth source. I got back into my car and headed home.

I have learned from bitter experience these last two years, that the Board of Education does not honor our collective bargaining agreement at all, and that the union's role in helping is that of a paper tiger in a bureaucratic jungle.

The union makes appointments with superintendents, locates lost paychecks, sends out letters, assigns personnel to escort grievants to hearings, and tries to keep them calm under fire from supervisors' attack but actually it has no power.

The Board of Education considers the teacher automatically the guilty party in any dispute, even though it is the teacher who is bringing charges against an administrator.

The contract is a declaration of war, a complete farce. I have devoted time energy, and interest to union activities. I was the only woman among the seven teachers who struck for collective bargaining back in 1960, thereby helping to start the union. Throughout these last ten years, I've attended meetings, rallies, conferences, emergency briefings, acted as a delegate, gone to Albany, and to Memphis to further union ideals. I have telephoned and wired legislators, picketed at every strike, distributed union literature at subway entrances, and in general, consider myself a very active and loyal U.F.T. member.

To my horror, I find my principal at Far Rockaway High School can threaten me, harass me, load my file with solicited letters from selected students, write an excoriating letter about me to the medical division, lie about me, mark me an unsatisfactory teacher on the basis of my response to all the previously mentioned abuses, and the union can do nothing. The union has led me, step by step, through the contractual stairway towards eventual arbitration, which is the only possible place where a teacher might get a chance to receive an impartial decision.

Yes, the union field representatives have been very kind to me, and the union grievance director has lunched with me and offered empathy, and the union lawyer has assured me that I am being completely supported to the best of their ability. But it is all meaningless, and empty, and cruel, because they fight a paper war, where the teacher is degraded and humiliated, week after week, and month after month. They really know that they have very little power, and that the teacher seldom gets a fair shake. The union, in a sense, sets the teacher up for the battle, and escorts her to Livingston Street, where the hatchetmen get paid to mete out despair and injustice. The union does not exist, in reality.

A few days later, a meeting was held in Mr. Gordon's office to discuss the pantyhose incident. As usual, his stony-faced expression was visible, carrying that set expression that forecast the tenor of the meeting about to take place.

Bob Arnesen began the discussion by asking where Mrs. Ashepa was. He pointed out that most of this meeting would be a protest against her handling of the incident. The principal stated that he felt her presence at this meeting was unnecessary, as she had told him everything. Bob voiced his objection to her non-appearance, then went on to ask that the whole incident be forgotten and also that Mrs. Ashepa be censured by the principal for her nasty remarks to me.

At the mere hint that Mrs. Ashepa had been at fault, Mr. Gordon squirmed in his chair, and bristled with anger. "This is a very serious matter, Mr. Arnesen, he said. Mrs. Ashepa tried to speak to Miss Newman, and Miss Newman insulted her. And Miss Newman exhibited herself to the class, and showed very poor judgment in this whole thing. She lost control of the class and caused great embarrassment to the students and the two assisting teachers, too."

We were shocked by his version of what had happened. He was taking, verbatim, what Mrs. Ashepa had carefully chosen to tell him and he completely omitted the fact that she had called me "the laughing stock of the school" and "sick, sick, sick." When he used

40

the term "exhibited herself," Bob interrupted to say that what had happened to me was an act of God and could have happened to anyone.

"Mr. Gordon, he said, didn't you every hear of a man's zipper opening accidentally, without his being aware of it? It's happened to me and it's happened to friends of mine, too. When the fact is called to your attention by someone, you simply zip up and go on with whatever you may have been doing."

Mr. Gordon glared at Bob, as though he had said something terrible, and completely ignored his remarks. It was as though he had never said a word. Then he reiterated that he was going to have to "do something" about me. He added that he had in his possession written statements from Mrs. Husten and Mrs. Cohen, the two assisting teachers, and was going to use them, "at the proper time."

We asked to see these statements and were refused. We asked what was in the statements and why they were written. Again, we were refused any information. An infuriating one-sidedness could be felt in the atmosphere.

Bob suggested that a meeting of the entire girls' health education department be held to bring the truth of the matter into the open. He said he felt that Mr. Gordon was not being fair to me, and that he hoped we would get a two-sided view at an open, well-attended meeting. He said that unless we got a fair settlement of this, our only recourse would be to file a formal Step One Grievance.

Mr. Gordon said he would hold the requested meeting on the following Thursday afternoon. The changing bell rang then, and freed us from the unpleasant session.

This underlying theme runs through this book, dear reader, but it could not be otherwise. You see, I keep clinging to the fantasy that I live in America where I am entitled to be heard; where the Bill of Rights permits free speech to all persons, not just principals and superintendents and supervisors. All my life I've believed that there are two sides to everything, and that in my wonderful, precious country, a person is innocent until proven guilty.

But this is not observed at Board of Education proceedings. Nowhere in my many journeys to superintendents' offices in Queens, and in Brooklyn, to the Chancellor's office, or to the Medical Director's office, did I ever get the feeling of a state of impartiality prevailing. A climate of disdainful tolerance filled the rooms, with false smiles and supercilious undertones abounding. I could retch as I type this, remembering.

Mr. Gordon cancelled the proposed Thursday meeting, without notifying either Bob or me. When Bob found out from the principal's secretary, he asked Mr. Gordon to come out of his office, to explain his arbitrary decision.

"I've decided there would be no point to holding the meeting, since Miss Newman is impossible to deal with," was Mr. Gordon's answer.

Bob voiced a protest at this and was told that the principal was "busy" and that he should leave the office.

Bob came and told me about this latest development and agreed that we should sit right down and compose the formal request for a Step One Grievance meeting, immediately. We did this and placed the request for the hearing in Mr. Gordon's letterbox.

The principal was now going to be the judge and hearing officer at this grievance meeting, as well as the defendant. Yes, that's right. And in all the three grievances I filed against this principal, he was both the hearing officer and the accused, at the same time.

Fair? Unbelievable? Well, that is the way the contract is set up. That is how the U.F.T. gets grievances resolved. That is the only way the teacher can even file a charge. Unbelievable? No, true!

I went about my normal routines and tried to tell as many of the faculty as I could what was going on. Some of my colleagues seemed interested, and also told me that they thought the whole thing was being distorted on purpose, because I had dared to speak up in my own behalf.

The date was now November 14, 1969, some two weeks after that fateful day in the gym. I was checking my letterbox contents, before leaving for the day. There it was in the familiar, unsealed white envelope. The principal had placed a letter about the pantyhose in my file, and this was my copy of it.

Chapter Five

Her Pantyhose Arrived at The Chancellor's office, Ten Months Later

HER PANTYHOSE ARRIVED AT THE CHANCELLOR'S OFFICE, TEN MONTHS LATER

It was a very clever piece, worded to give the reader the impression that the teacher sat there, with her legs in a wide-apart position, for the entire period. The implication that the reader would draw was that this was done deliberately. Actually, as I have shown, the whole incident took about two minutes, and at the very moment that I noticed the tear, I covered it with my hand, but no mention is made of that in this letter.

"Dear Miss Newman:

It has come to my attention that on Wednesday, October 29, 1969, your pantyhose were torn at the crotch while you were demonstrating. Nevertheless, you continued to demonstrate to the students. What made the situation even more acute was the fact that you were not wearing underpants, and the students and your assistants were very conscious of this fact.

We all understand that accidents of this sort occur. May I suggest, however, that in a case like this it would be proper for you to turn the conduct of the class over to one of your assistants in order to make necessary personal adjustments. This would avoid any embarrassment to you and to the students, and would spare everyone the awkward reaction that tends to occur.

We all realize the gym floors require special care, and street shoes should not be used. I have spoken to you about this, but am taking the opportunity of mentioning it once again, since it is department policy."

I was signed by the acting chairman.

As I read it the second time, I could feel anger well up within m at the nastiness of this latest gesture of the administration. Seeing Bob at the time clock, I rushed over to him and showed the letter to him. He read it and shook his head, slowly, as he said that he felt it was a rotten thing to do and that it was obviously designed to give a false and damning impression of me.

We also realized that the last paragraph about my wearing street shoes in the gym was added purposely, even though it did not actually fit into the context of the complaint against me, to make it seem as though I were a teacher who did not follow department policy. Obviously, any intelligent and fair-minded person who knew me would realize that I would not have remained a member of the department had I not been familiar with and adhered to department policy.

Bob advised me to sign one copy immediately and he offered to take it to Mr. Gordon's office for me. I thanked him and also asked that he inform Mr. Gordon that we were filing for a Step One Grievance immediately. Before punching out for the day, Bob also offered to notify Mr. Speranza at U.F.T. headquarters, that a letter had been placed in my file.

A few days later, a Step One Grievance meeting took place in the principal's office. It was a meaningless, humiliating scene, because Mr. Gordon simply would not listen to anything that the chapter chairman or I had to say.

He kept insisting that he had all the facts, and that Mrs. Ashepa had acted properly in speaking to me the way she did, as she was a supervisor. He also reiterated that he was going to do everything he could to see that I be removed from the classroom, since I was a terrible teacher.

I reminded him that he had not been present in the gym when I had my accident, and that everything he was saying was a result of hearsay, since Mrs. Ashepa was not present, either, when the tear occurred. Bob then reminded him that he had never observed me teach a class even though I had invited him to do so.

When we received the formal note from Mr. Gordon, a few days later, informing me of the reasons why he was denying my grievance appeal. I was not surprised by the verdict.

As soon as Bob read the denial note, he drafted a Step Two appeal letter for me to type up at home, and mail to the high school superintendent's office. I took care of this unpleasant chore the moment I arrived home.

Superintendent Dorothy B. Kole wrote back that we were to appear before her on December 3, 1969, for a formal Step Two hearing at her office, at Board of Education headquarters.

About two weeks later, Bob Arnesen, Tom Pappas, the district coordinator for the U.F.T., and I were ushered into a small office, filled with smoke. Mr. Gordon was already there. The secretary took us to the Superintendent's desk as the rear of the room. The desk was a disaster area piled high with paper, folders, and letters. It looked as though all the office file cabinets had just toppled over and spilled out their contents. The Superintendent was puffing away on a cigarette, held captive in a long holder. A stately, imperious woman, she looked us over, intently, and motioned us to chairs arranged around her desk.

Tom had instructed me to tell my story exactly as it had happened, and to try to remain calm, no matter what was said. I promised to try.

I was surprised, then disgusted, when Mrs. Kole turned to Mr. Gordon, who had come here alone, and said, "Mr. Gordon, I know we're supposed to conduct a Step Two hearing today, but I haven't been able to find your letter and I must confess that I don't remember what this grievance is all about. As briefly as you can, please give me the essential details and we'll get on with it."

She hardly acknowledged our presence. Since it was I who had filed the grievance against Mr. Gordon, and not the reverse, common courtesy would dictate that the grievant be heard first. Immediately afterward, she could then ask the principal for his counter-argument. But that did not happen, at this hearing, or at any other hearing I later attended.

Mr. Gordon began by stating very emphatically that Miss Newman had created a very serious state of affairs in the school, by her handling of the pantyhose matter. He pointed out that these were the facts of the matter, and that, in effect, nothing else could possibly be said, by Miss Newman, or Mr. Arnesen or Mr. Pappas or anyone else. Mrs. Ashepa had told him everything, he reaffirmed, and he was satisfied that he knew all the facts. Miss Newman had committed a serious error of judgment by continuing to demonstrate to her class while her private parts were in full view.

Superintendent Kole kept nodding her head, after each of Mr. Gordon's pronouncements, as though she was in complete accord with him.

Tom and Bob raised objections to the manner in which Mr. Gordon was conveying the details to her, but Superintendent Kole waived their statements out of the minutes, by motioning to the stenotypist to ignore the statements. She allowed Mr. Gordon to finish speaking.

I also attempted to butt in, to challenge the principal's statements, but Mrs. Kole asked me to remain quiet, in a tone a mother might use to silence a bothersome child. Her attitude remained condescending and disdainful towards me throughout the afternoon's proceedings, while she fawned all over Mr. Gordon. It was sickening, but since I experienced this same kind of double approach at subsequent hearings, with other Board of Education officers, I can only conclude that this is standard procedure in grievance hearings. The principal is right, no matter what the facts may actually be, and the grievant is tolerated, and listened to in a half-hearted way, to give the impression that there is a chance that right will prevail.

When our side of the matter was finally sought by Superintendent Kole, Tom Pappas raised objections to Mr. Gordon's testimony, declaring that it was all opinion, not fact. He pointed out that neither Mr. Gordon nor Mrs. Ashepa was present in the gymnasium when my pantyhose tore, and so their views were based on hearsay and rumor, rather than eyewitness account.

"Superintendent Kole," Tom continued. "We also object to Mrs. Ashepa's absence today. Her remarks to Miss Newman and the fact that her signature appears on this nasty letter are crucial aspects of this meeting. She should be here."

Mr. Gordon argued that he knew all the facts, and could handle this meeting alone.

Tom asked for a two-minute recess, so that we three could leave the room, and decide how to proceed. We decided to continue the hearing now, rather than have it postponed to some future date, arbitrarily set by Mrs. Kole. We re-entered the room and said we would continue, but under protest. We asked that the protest be recorded in the minutes.

"All right, let's go on, now," Superintendent Kole ruled. "Mr. Pappas, I'll hear your statements now."

Tom spoke clearly and rapidly and did his best to have the letter removed from my file. "We feel this whole matter has been blown up and distorted out of proportion," he said. "and that this has been done quite deliberately by both Mr. Gordon and Mrs. Ashepa. This letter presents a distorted version of what actually happened. The way the letter is written, one gets the impression that Miss Newman made no attempt to cover herself, or to correct the situation in as professional a manner as she could. It also is made to appear that Miss Newman was sitting there with her legs apart for a full period when the whole incident, from the time the teacher herself noticed the tear, to the time that she stood up, lasted approximately two minutes."

"I have asked Miss Newman to bring to this meeting, today, the pantyhose that she was wearing on October twenty-ninth so that you could see the actual tear, and realize it was the right crotch region with which we are concerned, rather than the crotch itself."

Tom handed the pantyhose to her as we watched, she held them up to the light and stretched them in several directions, before handing them back.

"Miss Newman," she said to me, quite harshly, "how can I be sure that these are the actual pantyhose you wore that day?"

I was flabbergasted by the question and was about to make a strong reply, but Tom, sensing my shock, answered in a voice brimming over with disgust. "Miss Newman is a professional person, a teacher with integrity, and you'll just have to take her word that these are the very same pair that she wore that day."

Bob Arnesen, sitting there taking in every word, seemed glad that Tom was doing most of the talking and, I assumed, at this early stage of my nightmare, that he was going to take an active role in my defense. After all, the chapter chairman is supposed to protect the teacher. It took me many months to see that Bob was timid, and like peace and quiet, even at the expense of justice to the grievant. He tried to be on both sides of the fence at the same time. His voice, in the teacher's lounge at school, was strong, and full of leadership tones, but whenever we were face-to-face with the principal, or other Board of Education people, it quivered with apology for trying to help the teacher. I didn't realize, until months later that he was afraid for himself and his position at Far Rockaway High School. I can say the same things about the assistant chapter chairman, Abe Gerewitz. He too, was always telling me to calm down and remain composed, as abuse upon abuse was heaped upon me by the administration. I mistook these comments for concern for me; in actuality, these men were really trying to protect themselves from future administrative wrath.

Tom held up a Random House dictionary, which he had brought with him, and suggested to the Superintendent that she look up the definition of the word "crotch" and make her decision now on what exact term would go into the minutes of the case.

Mrs. Kole glared at Tom, and retorted that she had already decided that the term "crotch" rather than "crotch area" would be the official one.

She then turned to me and asked "Miss Newman, how long have you been teaching and how long at Far Rockaway High School?"

When I replied that I had taught for more than twenty years, and that most of that time, sixteen years, was spent at Far Rockaway High School, she looked at me intently and said one word, but it was loaded with disdain. "Really." was her comment. "Let's go on, then. What have you to add to this meeting?"

I poured out the whole story in a calm, sequential way, so that there could be no misinterpreting of what I had done that day. I stressed the fact that I had taught the very same class the next day, and things were normal and routine and that no students had asked me anything about the previous day. I objected to Mrs. Ashepa's remarks to me, especially the name-calling and the "sick, sick, sick" bit.

Mrs. Kole stared at me in an appraising fashion. She seemed to be listening to what I was saying. But when she turned away, abruptly, and questioned Mr. Gordon in that saccharine tone I had become accustomed to hear when a supervisor was being addressed, I couldn't help wincing.

"Would you like to add anything, now, before I ask any of my own questions, Mr. Gordon?" she asked.

He scowled at me as he answered her. "I feel it is very important for you to know that when Mrs. Ashepa tried to talk to Miss Newman, quietly, about the incident Miss Newman called her supervisor a 'bitch'. I consider this highly improper."

Tom waived his hand in the air and insisted on being heard. The Superintendent allowed his comment.

"Mr. Gordon," he laughed out. "It is Mrs. Ashepa who made highly improper remarks to Miss Newman first, and it is she who should be disciplined, not Miss Newman. If any supervisor had spoken to me the way Mrs. Ashepa spoke to Fran, I'd have done a lot more than just answer back. A punch in the mouth would have been more appropriate."

Mrs. Kole sat there, eyes cast down at her desk, in quiet reflection. She seemed about to answer Tom, but instead ignored him completely, and turned back to Mr. Gordon.

"Mr. Gordon, what were your other sources of information about the incident?" she asked.

"In addition to the two statements I showed you, from Mrs. Cohen and Mrs. Husten, Miss Newman's assistants, the chairman of the boys' health education department told me that his wife told him that some girls told her of the incident" was Mr. Gordon's response.

I thought surely Superintendent Kole would say something about all this hearsay testimony, but she seemed to accept it all, and indeed, made no comment whatsoever about it.

"Is that all?" she asked. "I think I've heard enough to reach a decision in this case."

"Superintendent Kole, there is one faculty member who came to me to report the incident, said Mr. Gordon. She is Miss Georges, a member of our Art Department. She told me some girls had talked to her about Miss Newman."

I gasped in disbelief. Helen Georges was the one teacher in the whole school who was really friendly and empathetic towards me. I looked at Bob for some kind of support and he motioned for me to remain quiet. I could not contain myself, and stood up to protest against Mr. Gordon's lie about Helen Georges. But Mrs. Kole brushed me aside and asked me to sit down.

"I have heard enough now," she said. "I do not need to hear any more. My decision will be mailed out, within the time period prescribed by the contract. "Good day!"

We were thus dismissed from her presence. She turned her back toward me. The whole afternoon was an exercise in futility, accompanied by a climate of partiality. I ran out of the room as I could feel the tears coming.

Tom and Bob caught up to me at the elevator and tried to comfort me on the short ride down. They suggested we all have a cup of coffee before plunging into the rush-hour traffic. As we entered a nearby luncheonette, my tears were replaced by a tight, knotted-up feeling throughout my body.

The two men felt as I did. They were not optimistic about the decision and felt that Mrs. Kole was too friendly towards Mr. Gordon to render a fair decision. She had been the installing officer at the ceremony welcoming Mr. Gordon to Far Rockaway. I had completely forgotten that detail, but now it loomed up, in all our memories, and forbode further ill.

Both men agreed that I should look for Helen Georges first thing in the morning and tell her how Mr. Gordon used her name at the hearing. They were certain, as was I, that she would confront him, face-to-face, and demand a retraction.

So, a few minutes later, the three of us started on our long trek home, through the nerve-jangling rush-hour traffic scene.

The next morning, Helen came over to my table in the corner and asked, "Well, how did it go, Fran? What do you think? What did Mr. Gordon say? What did Mildred Ashepa say?" Her questions streamed forth, and I knew she would be shocked at my response.

"Helen, dear, sit down and listen," I began. "Let me tell you the whole thing, in sequence. You'll understand why in a minute or two."

She sipped her coffee, and listened. When I told her that Mr. Gordon had testified that she was one of the teachers who had reported me to him, she dropped her cup, and spilled coffee onto the table. She looked horrified. "Whaaat! How dare he use my name? I never spoke to him. I never went near his office. What a lousy trick to pull. I'm going right up to his office and tell him a thing or two. What nerve! See you at lunch."

Dashing out of the cafeteria, she nearly bowled over a teacher who was trying to enter. I sat there by myself a few minutes longer, pondering the scene that was about to take place in the principal's office.

The day wore on and suddenly it was lunch time. I rushed down to the cafeteria to look for Helen. She was already seated. I selected the nearest sandwich and ran to her table. Abe Gerewitz, the union chapter chairman, was at the table, too. He welcomed me, and moved his tray aside to give me more room.

"I spoke to Mr. Gordon, Helen said, and he tried to brush me off with the remark that he only casually threw my name in. He said it was nothing to be concerned about and he advised me not to get involved in your affairs. He assured me that he didn't mean to upset me." "Well, I let him have it, Fran. I told him he had no right to use my name in testimony against a teacher who happens to be a friend of mine, or at any time, without my permission. Boy, what nerve."

Abe looked quite startled. He said Mr. Gordon had no right to lie at the hearing, and was upset that the principal would stoop so low.

I thanked Helen for doing what she did and asked her if she would put her story in writing to me. I told her that I probably would have to file a Step Three appeal, and that her letter stating that Mr. Gordon had lied and had used her name at a formal Step Two hearing, would be very helpful.

We talked then about telling as many of the faculty as we could, since the same thing could be done to them. I asked Abe to discuss the possibility of handling a special U.F.T. chapter meeting, so I could speak to the teachers about what was happening to me.

During the next ten days, I kept checking the mail, looking eagerly for Superintendent Kole's decision. When I finally arrived I tore open the envelope. The decision was against me.

Unbelievable? Outrageous? I think so.

Chapter Six

Death and Hypocrisy
Enter The Nightmare

DEATH AND HYPOCRISY ENTER THE NIGHTMARE

Death hovered about my home from January, 1969 until the evening of October 10. 1969, when the final blow was dealt. My mother succumbed to the brain tumor that had been invading her vital centers for those long, heartbreaking months, rendering her completely helpless.

My father and sister and I were agonized by the progress of the condition, because we were forced to watch a lovely, voluptuous, energetic woman slip into an unrecognizable being. There was no resemblance between the wasted form on that hospital bed and the warm, vibrant personality who was my mother.

The top neurologist and surgeon at Flower Fifth Avenue Hospital had correctly diagnosed mother's symptoms almost immediately, and since my father is a physician, we were given the actual medical details as well, and there was no escaping the bitter reality that she would die shortly. The doctors did everything they possible could to make mother comfortable, and suggested that we place her in a hospital where she could receive the very best care all the way to the terminal point of her illness. They recommended St. Barnabas Hospital in the Bronx, and within a few days we were lucky to be able to secure a bed for her there.

Mother shared a room with a little old lady who was senile, and who chattered away all day about all kinds of things, and thereby livened up the room, which, to us who came there each day to visit, was a very grim place. Many friends and relatives visited both the little old lady and my mother, so that there was a constant flow of voices and kind words and laughter, which helped dispel the gloom. The practical nurses were in constant attendance, too, and this added to the patient's and the patient's family's feeling of security.

Our only comforting thought at the bitter end, when mother died, was the fact that she felt no pain, and really did not know what was happening to her. At the last moment, she was in a deep sleep, and simply could not be roused by the evening attendant, who had come into the room with her dinner tray.

I stayed home for a few days, mourning our loss with my very large family. Aunts, uncles, cousins, neighbors and innumerable friends came to my father's house to pay the customary condolence call, and to help us to bear the pain of our loss. We all bemoaned the unfairness of my mother's kind of final illness. She had been a beautiful woman, who took very good care of herself, and who looked 50 although she had reached her seventieth year, when she was struck down by the tumor. Her illness ravaged her so completely and changed her into a totally different Adele, who loved to laugh and dance and bake and hug her grandchildren, and who worried about everybody.

When the Shiva period of mourning was over, I returned to school. I entered the gym for my afternoon class and was shocked when one of my students came up to me and asked "What are you doing back here, Miss Newman?" "What do you mean, dear?" I asked the student. "My mother passed away last week and I stayed home for the usual period of mourning. Is there something unusual about that?"

The student averted her eyes for a moment, and then said quickly, "We were told that you had been fired and were not coming back."

I was taken aback by this remark. "Who told you this?" I asked her.

The girl looked at me and said that she thought it was Mrs. Jacobs who had told her. Mrs. Jacobs was a member of the department who had taken my class in my absence.

The more I thought about the statement, the more I was determined to track down its source. I decided to tell Bob Arnesen, the chapter chairman, about what the student said had been told to my class.

He was also shocked at the statement, and felt that it should not have been made, and agreed with me that it was unprofessional, and even vicious. But he didn't want to do anything about it, except to forget it. So I determined to try to ferret out the truth by sifting through and following up any information.

At lunch the next day, I mentioned the remark to a young male teacher from the distributive education department, to see what he thought about it. He was stunned and said he had heard from another teacher in his department, within the last few days, that some students in her class had told her that I had been fired. She had asked these girls which teacher had told them this, and they said, too, that it had been Mrs. Jacobs.

I asked Mike to get the specifics from the woman teacher, as I wanted to be sure of my facts before I accused Mrs. Jacobs. Mike suggested that I come up to his department and see her personally, so I agreed and told him to tell her I'd be up during my afternoon free period.

When I arrived there, later in the day, I looked for Mrs. Gottlieb, the teacher to whom the girls had spoken, and found her in one of the typing rooms. She told me that some of the students in her class had been talking about me, and about the fact that I had been fired. When she asked them how they came to know this, they said the teacher who was covering Miss Newman's class had told them. She took out her Delaney book and looked through it for the names of the girls who had actually spoken to her.

"Fran, I can't remember exactly which kids had told me this. Do you recognize any of these names?" she asked, holding up the large book for me to look through. None of the names seemed familiar. "These names don't ring a bell with me, I said, so would you look over the class again, and let me know, say tomorrow. O.K?" She readily agreed to check her class the next day.

The following day, Mrs. Gottlieb greeted me coldly, and said she couldn't remember who had told her that I had been fired. Would I please forget the whole thing? She told me that she didn't want to get involved in my problems, and would rather that I not bother her again.

Disgusted with her attitude, I left her room. Later, when I told Mike about it, he said she was probably scared and decided to back out. Bob Arnesen advised me to drop the whole thing, as he felt I would be very difficult to pinpoint who had actually said what and when and to whom.

I decided to put this aside, temporarily, and probably would have allowed it to recede into the depths of my memory, but as you know from the previous two chapters, the pantyhose incident occurred around this time, and the harassment began again, in full blast.

First, a condolence card was sent to my father's home, after my mother's death, by Mr. Gordon. I read it, with my dad present, and became so upset, I almost cried. "That lousy hypocrite," I cried out to my father. "He's harassing me to death at school, makes all kinds of threats and charges and sets up that kangaroo court, and now he sends me a card. What a horrible phony he is! I feel like throwing this card in his face."

My dad understood my distress and said it would be best to ignore the card. "Make believe it never arrived. It would have been more honest not to send a card at all, and simply overlook or ignore the fact that your mother had died. But with this kind of despot, this is what you can expect."

I agreed with his comments, and threw the card in the waste basket, unanswered. Going through the stack of condolence cards, I came upon a small envelope with the American Cancer Society address at the top left hand corner. The sender's address was stamped on the back flap: "Girls' Health Education Department, Far Rockaway High School."

So they had sent a phony message, too. They had co-operated with Mildred Ashepa at the phony kangaroo court proceedings last March, and were fawning all over this female bully, and now they were sending me a note saying how sorry they were that I had lost my mother. And they compounded their rottenness by making a donation, in my mother's name, to the Cancer Society.

"Dad, read this from my department. It's such a low thing to do. They chip in fifty cents a piece to make a contribution in mother's name, and it makes them look good. I think it's positively indecent."

Dad read the card, and then tossed it in the wastebasket, as he declared, "Yes, dear. They are a bunch of rotten hypocrites. I quite agree with you. It belongs in the garbage pail with the other one."

"Listen, dad, I'm going to call the Cancer Society in the morning and ask them to send that check back to those phonies. I'll tell them that I'll double the contribution so their quota will not be affected and tell them my reason for wanting the money returned. I don't want these teachers even remotely involved with our tragedy. Their gestures are completely unwelcome to me, dad. Any objection on your part?"

"No, Fran. I share your feelings in this matter. Take care of it in the morning, and then try not to give the matter another thought. They are not worth one more tear. I am outraged at the way you're being treated by that principal. I'm seriously thinking of writing a letter to the newspapers and to the Governor and to the Mayor and anyone else who can help. You just give me the word and I'll act. Meanwhile, dear, let's try to answer as many of these condolence cards as we can now. I find this task very painful and tiring, and I'm sure you feel the same way."

I agreed with my father that we should get on with this grim but necessary work. The fact that so many people were paying tribute to my mother's memory made the job a little easier, and lessened the awful impact her death had on us.

A few weeks later, several events took place at the school directly related to the way the pantyhose incident was handled by Mr. Gordon and Mrs. Ashepa. Helen Georges, the art teacher, wrote the letter that she had promised to write:

December 9, 1969

"To whom it may concern:

It has come to my attention that my name was used by Mr. Gordon at a Step Two Grievance instituted by Miss Newman.

I was astonished and a bit indignant to hear this. At no time was I consulted about the incident in question, asked for any information, or informed that my name would be used in a manner relating to the incident.

If I was mentioned in the capacity of a complainant or witness, the statement was erroneous and improper.

If I was mentioned as one who was and is aware of the incident, that statement was true.

I am aware of the incident.

I heard about it from Miss Newman.

Sincerely,

(Miss) Helen Georges

I thanked Helen for writing the letter and showed it to everyone with whom I came in contact. It was an excellent letter, and I was sure it would help me at Step 3.

Many teachers came up to the faculty lounge and looked at the poster I placed there, about the entire pantyhose incident. The traffic on the back stairway leading to that room was very heavy. I spent my preparation period in the lounge each day, and teachers would comment and commiserate with me, but no one offered to help. Several teachers told me how cruel and mean Mr. Gordon had been to them, but they confessed to me, as though their gutlessness was some kind of virtue, that they didn't choose to fight back. They said they admired me for fighting back, so I suggested that they file grievances, too, so there would be a lot of complaints against Mr. Gordon at headquarters. It would be clear to all what a despicable, weak and incompetent man he was, and maybe something could be done about him.

Here are some of the other teacher's complaints:

Mrs. Garcia, a grade adviser, had prepared a program for a boy in her group. Later, when the students had checked into their subject classes, and the program cards were checked by the grade adviser, Mrs. Garcia found that this boy had changed his program card by erasing the original class assignments, and writing in his own choices. She called this student to her office, and during the interview, it was quite evident from the boy's manner and evasiveness, that he had indeed forged his program. Mrs. Garcia changed the program back to what it was, originally, and warned the boy not to do this kind of thing again. She made an entry on his master card in her office, and let the matter drop there.

To her surprise, and disgust, a few weeks later, she was called into the principal's office, to discuss a letter from the boy's mother, who charged her with being mean and unfair to her son. When Mrs. Garcia tried to explain, and asked that the boy be brought in to this discussion, Mr. Gordon refused to listen, and let her know that he considered the mother's charge a very serious one and he was going to bear this in mind. She left the office in tears, but, at the same time, did nothing about it. If she had filed a grievance, and aired the facts of the matter, perhaps this tyrant would tread a little lighter.

A speech teacher, who had been at the school for more than twenty years, and was fully licensed in that subject area, had been assigned by Mr. Gordon to teach regular English classes instead of her own specialty. The speech program was given to a brand new substitute teacher, who also had the license but lacked experience. Mrs. Mines protested to her chairman, and then to Mr. Gordon. His response to her constitutes, in my opinion, a grossly improper and unprofessional act.

"Mrs. Mines," the principal said to her, in his somber and cold way, "The reason I'm not having those classes assigned to you is that the Puerto Rican students hate you. Is that clear?"

I asked her to file a grievance, and to join me, in seeing that attention be focused on this man, so that he could be stopped. Since we have a grievance machinery built into the collective bargaining agreement, I urged her to use it.

She refused, saying that she admired me for trying to fight back, but she excused herself from playing an active role in her own defense, and thereby, in all other teachers' defense, by saying she didn't have the strength to fight. She fully supported me in my desire to bring charges against Mr. Gordon, of harassment and inequitable treatment, but she would do nothing to help me, because she didn't have the strength to get involved. I walked away from her, in disgust.

Meanwhile, the day after I placed the poster in the teacher's lounge, it disappeared. I was asked by some teacher who had heard about it, if I had removed it. I said that I had no idea who had taken it. After scouting around, Bob Arnesen, the chapter chairman, learned that Mr. Gordon had been seen entering the lounge, later in the same day, so we could surmise that he had removed the poster. We felt he had no right to do this, as the teacher's room was used only by the faculty, and it certainly is no crime for a teacher to tell other teachers what was happening to her at the school. After all, the school was on triple session, and it was very difficult, indeed, to see everyone on the staff. So, after talking it over with Bob, I decided on the poster, and printed newsletters, at my own expense, as the proper vehicles for disseminating the course of events.

A few days later, at lunch with Abe, he told me of a letter that had been sent to the U.F.T., by my department. He was informed by Mr. Gordon, himself, that Miss Newman's entire department had signed this particular letter against her, and that he, the principal, took this as further proof of the fact that Miss Newman was a terrible teacher and should be gotten rid of, as quickly as possible. When Abe questioned Mr. Gordon for facts and further details, Mr. Gordon said, openly, and definitely, that he was going to do everything in his power to have me removed from the New York City system. He had decided that I was an awful person, and despite a good record and many commendations along the way, from former chairman and principals, he had decided that I should not be teaching. Abe told me this, and I was upset, naturally, but not shocked or stunned, as I had been at earlier meetings.

"Did he show you the letter?" I asked angrily. "Did you ask for a copy of the letter?" Abe shook his head, and said he was sure I could see the letter at U.F.T. headquarters, and that he tried to escape from Mr. Gordon's presence before he said anything he might later regret.

My lunch, suddenly, no longer interested me, and as I arose from the table, I asked Abe to tell Bob about the letter, and to also try to arrange for a U.F.T. meeting, so that I could speak to the members, and appeal to them for some kind of protest against all this.

I ran up the stairs, and headed for the phones. I quickly reached my U.F.T. field representative. Charles Loiacono, who said, "Yes, Fran, I have the letter right here. It's awful. I think those women in your department are a rotten lot. Come on down and you can read it, but don't let it get you. They're not worth it, and anyone who can sign such a letter, is a vicious person and probably scared of the principal, and thinks nothing of selling out a department member, to save her own skin."

When I arrived at the grievance office, Charlie attempted to be cheerful and comforting, but I was very brusque with him, due to my impatience. I saw that he understood my feelings now, and he opened the folder on his desk, and extracted the letter.

As I read it, feelings of frustration, outrage and despair intermingled with bitterness, flowed furiously within me. I could feel my skin getting all prickly and hot as I read this slanderous and lying letter.

December 8, 1969

United Federation of Teachers
250 Park Avenue South
New York City, New York

Attention: Mr. Speranza
Mr. Pappas

Gentlemen:

Our Chapter Chairman is currently pursuing a grievance filed by Miss Francine Newman in regard to a letter which she wishes removed from her file.

We, her colleagues in the Women's Health Education Department, wish to present in the strongest possible terms, our conviction that your efforts are being misdirected. We consider that the letter, as filed, provides a completely fair and objective presentation of proven inexcusable and unprofessional conduct on the part of the alleged aggrieved.

The most effective contribution which the U.F.T. can make in this case to teacher morale and effective education is to support the department and union teachers. We, as dues paying and active U.F.T. members, demand that the interests of all the teachers and pupils not be sacrificed to the whim of one complainer, whose distorted sense of values has, for years, created serious educational and morale problems for her colleagues and pupils, as well as innumerable instances of parent and community friction which have reflected discredit on the department, the school and the entire New York City educational system.

Sincerely yours,

Helen Arum
Mildred Ashepa
Rosalie Beal

Ellen Dee Cohen
Marcia Jacobs
Carole Husten
Alice C. Nirenberg

The letter, besides being full of lies, is also a prime example of the hypocrisy surrounding me.

The following brief outline is the truth about what the letter says.

Mrs. Ellen Dee Cohen and Mrs. Carol Husten, are both young substitute teachers, who had just come into the Health Education Department. They could only have been dues paying U.F.T. members for about two weeks, because the Union was being penalized by the Taylor Law rulings, and no dues checkoff was being permitted. Neither of these two teachers ever appeared during the many weeks of the strike, to help out by picketing or attending meetings. Also, I had personally had conversations in the Health Education office with Mrs. Husten, in which she said she didn't believe in unions and that many of her friends in the Nassau schools had told her many terrible things about unions, etc., etc, ad nauseam. Since Mrs. Cohen and Mrs. Husten were brand new substitute teachers at Far Rockaway High School, how could they sign a letter that allegedly tells about my terrible actions all through the many preceding years?

Mrs. Marcia Jacobs lives across the street from the school, and never showed her face during the long, bitter weeks of our strike. On one occasion, a group of us walked over to her house to see if we could get her out to do some picketing duty, and to possibly let those of us out there in the street use her bathroom facilities. She acquiesced to the latter. In the two years or so that she had been a member of the department and school faculty, I had never seen her at any U.F.T. meeting. Yet she signed this letter, as a dues paying and active member. she set herself up as an authority to judge a teacher with fifteen years teaching experience in the same school when she was only a recent arrival!

Alice Nirenberg was a gym teacher who became Dean of Girls during Mr. Gordon's principalship. I had always thought of her as a friend, as well as colleague, whom I had invited to my home many times, had traveled with, had been a confidante during her several stays in the hospital, etc. and then all of a sudden, she's signing this letter against me. I have a letter in my file, from her, when she was Acting Dean, full of praise for me, about my creative gift and my contribution to the school.

I have at least ten letters of commendation from my previous department chairmen, Albert Rosenthal and Robert Rommer, commending me for my dedication to the department, for my creative bulletin boards, for volunteering for the pilot program in connection with the hygiene program, etc. and yet these teachers were willing to sign this letter for the principal. Why?

I might add that when the rest of the faculty were made aware of this letter later on, they verbally condemned the signers of it and I invited them to discuss this letter and how it came to be written, at a U.F.T. meeting, but not one of my department members showed up at the meeting, which took place the following month, after the Christmas recess.

I left the U.F.T. office feeling very despondent, and helpless, and these feelings have been with me these many months, as the web of lies and allegations became more and more tangled, making the path towards extricating myself from this horrible mess, more and more difficult.

January, 1970 brought with it, a darker cloud of gloom, under which I have been living since.

Chapter Seven

January Infamy

JANUARY INFAMY

Christmas vacation helped a lot to untangle my emotional knots, and it ended all too soon. I sunned and swam and conversed with other guests at the lovely resort hotel in Venezuela. Touring the city of Caracas and visiting the various historic points of interest there, and then coming back to the beautiful Hotel Tamanaco for a sumptuous dinner certainly helped my morale a great deal. But, all too soon, our flight director gathered us all together and did his best to herd his suntanned flock of teacher-tourists onto the chartered plane, waiting for us on the runway. Reluctantly, but realistically, I boarded the flight, and returned home to harassment and tension and an atmosphere of deception and betrayal.

January presents many opportunities for a teacher to work with faculty members other than those in her own department. Regents exam proctoring assignments, then the marking of these exams, and working on various end-term committees provide lots of time to see and talk to other teachers. I have always enjoyed working with other departments and thereby getting out of the sameness of the daily routine within my subject area. Many of my closest associates in school were members of the Social Studies, English, and Foreign Language departments, and so, at this time, every term, I could actually socialize with them as well as do all the work entailed in getting three thousand students into the proper classes, time schedules, with all their grades and recommendations and special needs, all properly accounted for. It is a tremendous overtaking, and has often reminded me of a gigantic female monster tied up in convulsive birth pains. After writhing and twisting and turning and groaning for three and a half weeks or so, she spews out her issue; three thousand programmed, graded and promoted or retained students, all set to dive into their new assignments. Her after-birth, of piles and piles of cards, records, papers, files, old programs, gets cleaned up by harried, frantic school clerks, and somehow all gets done. The confusion resulting from many clerical errors quiets down, usually, within ten days or so after the new term has started, and everything settles into routine.

I was glad this time had rolled around, and spent as little time as possible in my department office. I avoided any contact with Mrs. Ashepa and the other health education teachers. The mere sight and sound of them annoyed me, and for good reason. I lunched at some of the local eateries in town, and that helped provide a necessary change of scene for me each day. Just leaving the building for an hour relaxed me considerably.

I was looking forward to speaking to the U.F.T. members at the January meeting. Both chapter chairmen had agreed to provide time for me to present my whole problem to them, for their consideration. I was hoping, of course, that my colleagues would become incensed at the treatment that I was receiving from the principal and my department, and unanimously draw up some kind of action plan to stop it. I figured that their understanding and empathy for a fellow teacher would lead to a mass invasion of Mr. Gordon's office and a demand that he stop violating the Union contract and stop his intimidation and unfair treatment of me. I assumed that they would all put themselves in my shoes and realize that the same thing could happen to them. Any teacher is vulnerable to abuse from a vicious supervisor, and here was a perfect opportunity to prevent that from happening. Also, the contract belongs to everyone, and whenever one teacher's contractual rights are violated, it follows that all teacher's rights are also being attacked. Concerted action and protest could certainly prevent future ugly situations from occurring, in the first place.

Bob Arnesen, the chapter chairman, printed the agenda for this meeting early enough so that every teacher had ample time to attend it. The notices were placed in everyone's letterbox a week ahead and so everyone in the school knew that I would be speaking at this meeting, and could show their support and interest, by attending. A few teachers approached me in the faculty lounge and asked about current developments and said all kinds of things to me, which, in their contradictions between statements and actions to back up these statements, hurt me. One teacher, male, with whom I often lunched, through the years, said to me in front of a few other teachers, "Fran, this whole thing is unbelievable. I'm on your team, and Gordon can go to hell. Sock it to him! He deserves it." I answered to Alex, and thanked him for his comments, and then he lowered his voice and sad, "But, listen, Frannie, don't use my name in the front office. I'm not a well man." I looked at this man, and also at the faces of the several teachers sitting there who had heard Alex's follow-up statement. Noncommittal, indifferent expressions on every face. No one said anything. Pencils rushed across exam papers and Delaney cards flipped over from the black side to the red side, but no words came forth. I left the teachers' lounge, feeling severely let down.

Another morning of that same week, a woman teacher of home economics, whom I had always liked and respected for her genuineness, warmth, and sensitivity, came to me in the lounge, and quietly said, "Fran, I'm so sorry all this is happening to you. You're a good teacher, Mr. Gordon is a cruel and difficult man and has no right to do this to you or anyone else." I warmed at Ruth's remark, and was just about to thank her when she added: "Fran, I'm with you, all the way from left field." "Ruth," I said, "Left field is too far away. I need you up at home plate." She then hesitated, frowned, and said softly. "But I can't do anything, Fran. You know I haven't been too well."

My throat tightened, and I said nothing. I wanted to call her a jellyfish, a coward, or something analogous, but thought to myself, "What's the use?" and simply turned away.

A history teacher named Ben, who also was a lawyer, and a rather shrewd and outspoken man most of the time, came over to me a little while later, and asked me to step outside. He had something important to tell me. I agreed, thinking he had heard what Ruth had said to me, earlier, and perhaps he may have wanted to comment on it. Instead, I received another verbal shock in he form of, "Listen, Fran. I know you're going through a lot and maybe I can do something for you. I've got a good friend down at U.F.T. headquarters, named Bernie. He's in the grievance department and I'm going to speak to him, and see if he can help in some way.

I looked right at Ben, and tried to see a mien of genuine comradeship there. I wanted to see sincerity. I had laughed at this man's jokes many times, and lunched at his table, and I liked him. He was always well-informed about what was happening in the world, and was a bright, alive, kind of person, whose company was stimulating. I half-heartedly started to say, "Ben, it's very decent of you to offer to help me. God knows, I need it," but the words died on my lips, as Ben continued with his offer. "But before I make this call, Francine, I want you to promise me that you won't say anything to anybody about this. I don't want it known around the school that I'm doing this. I've only got a few years to go, and I don't want any trouble."

I felt tears forming in my eyes, and my throat tighten. I stood there, speechless, rooted to the spot, for a minute. Ben saw the look of despair and disgust, and walked away. We never spoke again. As I walked down the corridor, I decided not to go into the teacher's lounge any more. Three teachers with whom I had experienced warm camaraderie for fifteen years had dealt me such painful verbal blows, and I was disappointed, angry and saddened, all at once. I became terribly fatigued, and sleepless. All that the sun and fresh air had done to refresh and rejuvenate me, was becoming undone by so-called friends' gestures of so-called assistance and support. I decided to remain as aloof as possible from everyone, until the meeting on January 27.

So, I lugged all my gym cards and permanent records and Delaney cards and administrative memos with me, in a shopping bag, each day. I looked for an empty classroom, and finding one sat at the front desk and attended to all my clerical duties.

The day finally arrived for the chapter meeting. I went up to the large laboratory-classroom and chatted with Bob Arnesen, the chapter chairman, and Abe Gerewitz, who were hoping for a large turn-out. They suggested that I try to be calm, and to speak in a soft tone, so that I wouldn't get upset. I thought they were concerned about me, and so, thanked them, and tried to do just as they suggested. They promised to tell all they had heard Mr. Gordon say about me so that the chapter would have the whole background of the case.

It was an overflow crowd. Every seat was taken. Many latecomers lined up at the back of the room, squatted on the floor, and even sat on the lab sink up front. There was an excitement in the crowd, and this was mainly because it was the end of the term and everyone was getting new programs, time schedules, and socializing a lot more than usual, because of our flexible time assignments, during these weeks of the January reorganization. Staff changes due to marriages, pregnancy, retirement and transfers were taking place, and everyone participated in the gossip and rumor mill, at every available opportunity. We all enjoy knowing what's going on, but it has been my unfortunate experience that when there's trouble on the rumor mill "hot line," the ostrich attitude takes over and the staff buries its head in the nearby sandpile of noninvolvement and justice be damned.

This was the best attended chapter meeting I had ever witnessed, with the exception of those tension-ridden pre-strike meetings, when every teacher was trying to decide what to do. Bob and Abe announced to the 150 teachers that they were delighted to see so many members, and they evinced confidence that a lot of good would be accomplished. They asked for quiet, passed out agendas to those who had forgotten to bring their copies along, and settle down to the issue at hand.

Finally, after we had waded through various school issues that occur at the end of every term, in every high school, such as time schedules, class size, etc., it was my turn to speak. Abe prefaced his introduction of me by asking that everyone listen carefully, as some very nasty things were about to be revealed. He assured the group that both he and Bob Arnesen were on my side, and the he could attest to the truth of everything that I would say. He appealed to the teachers to decide for themselves what they wanted to do about this, since both he and Bob could verify that Mr. Gordon had been intimidating her for more than a year, now, and that a most unfair and unprofessional thing was being allowed to continue, and should not be.

I spoke to my colleagues, in a quiet, orderly fashion. I cited Mr. Gordon's handling of my complaints made against me by the mothers of Susan Reiner and Robin Feuerstein. Then I explained how the kangaroo court scene had come into existence the previous March. I went into great detail about the pantyhose incident, and how the letter in my file had come to be written by Mrs. Ashepa. There was a stirring in the group, and one of the assembled teachers raised his hand to ask a question. Bob called on him. The teacher looked around and then asked, "Why isn't Mrs. Ashepa here, too? Everybody who's involved in this mess should be here." Then everyone began looking around and buzzing about the whereabouts of my acting chairman and the other women in my department.

Not one of my department had come to the meeting. Bob and Abe told the crowd that these teachers knew about the meeting and were notified about the agenda, and that their absence, therefore, was significant. The chapter, he said, could draw its own conclusions. Abe asked me to continue, and I told them about the letter that my department had sent to the U.F.T. not to support me. There were lots of sounds coming from the group now, and it appeared that many of the teachers had not bothered to learn all the facts in my case, and were actually hearing some of the details for the first time. When I stressed the fact that two of the signees in the matter, Mrs. Cohen and Mrs. Husten, were substitutes, who had just recently come to the school, and hardly knew me, there was a visible reaction in the crowd.

I returned to my seat to await developments.

Lots of discussion went on, and the end result was a formal written protest by the U.F.T. members against the actions of Mr. Gordon:

> "As a result of an overflow meeting held in Room 261 on January 27 (which ran for over two hours) the following resolution was unanimously passed, delivered to the principal, and subsequently followed by a conference at which both parents exchanged positions.
>
> The U.F.T. Chapter wishes to go on record as condemning the methods used by the administration against individual members of the faculty which are creating an atmosphere of harassment, persecution and polarization; placing letters of complaint in the teacher's file weeks after an incident; acting upon hearsay evidence supplied by students and others; accepting anonymous sources of complaints; setting colleague against colleague, etc."

The Chapter also agreed to set up a faculty committee to handle intra-faculty disputes, and matters pertaining to harassment of teachers, etc., to prevent the same kind of thing from happening again.

I was glad that this action was taken, and hoped that things would quiet down and come to a halt. But my optimism was immediately squashed when Bob and Abe told me the principal's reaction to the letter of protest. He said, "I am not here to be liked."

Little did we know that even as we were holding this meeting on January 27th, Mr. Gordon had composed and mailed an excoriating letter about me, to Dr. Theodore Lang, chief of personnel, asking that I be given a psychiatric and medical examination as quickly as possible, since I was out of control and creating serious problems in the school.

This letter was dated January 26th, and had been mailed to my home, special delivery, in time to arrive early Saturday morning.

When I was awakened by the persistent ringing of my front doorbell, I jumped out of bed and found the postman there, with a big manila envelope, with my name on it. I tore open the envelope, and pulled out a sheaf of papers, and began pawing over the papers.

The horror of it all struck me, when the poster I had pasted up on the desk in the teachers lounge fell out of the envelope.

The chapter title I have assigned to these pages was born at that moment, but I didn't know that then.

Does it make sense, or resemble a fair procedure, to place the letters in the file, first, and honor the complaints therein, first, and then later, days or weeks later, send the teacher a copy of the letters, for her signature, after the fact. This was the principal's ugly technique.

Read on, and you'll meet the new tenants in my file, one by one, and perhaps you will understand my desire to get them all out, as soon as I knew of their occupancy.

My anger and frustration at the slowness and unfairness of the process involved in getting all these people out of my file, has been building up, for three years now.

The first letter was placed there, in March, 1970.

It is now January, 1973, and the letters are <u>still</u> in my file.

Chapter Eight

Malice Unlimited – From Bay 25ᵗʰ St.
to Court Street

MALICE UNLIMITED – FROM BAY 25TH STREET TO COURT STREET

Mr. Gordon had sent the letter, shown below, dated January 25, 1970 to Dr. Theodore Lang, Deputy Superintendent, and within a week, my whole life underwent a barrage of attacks, designed to wither and destroy me. Fortunately, the attacks on me strengthened my resolve to expose what was being done to me, deliberately, by David Gordon, with the co-operation and protection of the various Board of Education lackeys, whose sole function is to back up principals in their chosen actions.

January 26, 1970

Dr. Nathan Brown
Superintendent of Schools
110 Livingston Street
Brooklyn, N.Y. 11201

ATTENTION: Dr. Theodore Lang

Dear Sir:

After consultation with my assistant superintendent, and in accordance with the Bylaws of the Board of Education, I request that a physical and medical examination be given to Miss Francine Newman, a teacher assigned to Far Rockaway High School.

Attached herewith is a report giving the reasons for my request for this examination.

I have sent a copy of this letter, as well as a copy of the report to Miss Newman.

Very truly yours,

David Gordon
Principal

DG:JF
CC: Mrs. Kole
     Miss Newman

FAR ROCKAWAY HIGH SCHOOL
Far Rockaway, N.Y. 11691

The following are the reasons for my request for a physical and medical examination of Miss Francine Newman.

It is my opinion that Miss Francine Newman, a teacher of Health Education at this school requires medical help and at least temporary relief for her duties. She is embittered, hostile, and alienated from most of her colleagues. Her judgments in professional areas are unusual and inappropriate. Her handling of pupils had resulted in an inordinate number of complaints and nasty pupil reactions. I cite specific illustrations.

In the handling of her classes, she is unreasonable and arbitrary in some of her demands, but cannot be persuaded of her error through reasoned discussion. Several times she charged students with having forged medical notes without first investigating, berated them violently, and referred them for disciplinary action. The medical notes proved to be authentic. Upon being apprised of this her response was "Well, it looked like a child's handwriting." On one occasion, she gave a "U" in citizenship to approximately 75 students in a class of 90, and defended her action by saying "I warned them I would do so if they misbehaved." When the principal and Mr. Rommer, then her chairman, held a conference with her to discuss the mass "U" incident, she angrily stormed out of the office saying. "Give me a U".

Except for minimum communication required professionally, she speaks with no one in her department, and coldly and strongly rejects any friendly overtures. At the time of her mother's death, recently, she publicly characterized as "hypocritical" the faculty members who sent condolence cards.   When she learned that members of her department had sent a contribution in her mother's name to the Cancer Society, she telephone their headquarters and demanded that the money be returned to the donors, saying that she would replace the sum with a personal contribution.

She assigns assisting teachers in physical education classes to duties easily handled by a student and screams at them and at the pupils when the incur her displeasure. Mr. Rommer, at a meeting with her and others, tried to tell her that this was why her assistants were hesitant to approach her. In rapid succession she rejected his statement, then admitting to the screaming, and finally condoned it by saying "she gets over it soon".

She rejects every suggestion by her supervisor that her actions are other than perfect. Recently, she dismissed a class without allowing adequate time for dressing. As the girls hurried from the locker room to avoid lateness to the next class, one child fell and was hurt. Miss Newman's chairman spoke to her and suggested that as a matter of safety she allow the full seven minutes for dressing. She replied, "No one told me about the accident, and children fall on the stairs all the time, anyhow." The next day, she again dismissed this class late. On another occasion, when the chairman tried to engage her in quiet conversation for privacy, she moved away ten feet or more, saying that there was nothing Mrs. Ashepa had to say to her that couldn't be overheard by students.

When reports of complaints to the principal from various staff members (deans, chairmen, etc.) accumulated, a meeting was held with Miss Newman and eight or nine other members of the faculty in an effort to help her and to extend an offer of support and a plea for friendliness. She rejected them all and let the group know that her handling of school situations was right and that of the others wrong. She then filed a grievance against the principal charging harassment, even though her presence at the meeting was voluntary, and the whole thing arranged with her approval and that of her adviser, Mr. Arnesen (UFT chapter chairman). At this grievance (Step 2) she demanded to know specific names of complaining students. Everytime I referred to an incident, she picked it up in detail, described it in detail, and acted as though her behavior in each instance were completely justified and sound. For example, she told one girl in her class that the girl was sick, and the girl replied "Look who's talking." Again, during conferences an Open School Night, she mimicked a foreign-speaking parent.

When the principal sends her a note, no matter how innocuous or politely worded, she becomes irate and challenging – even though the note may merely request information. The accompanying note (Exhibit A) was sent to her. She asked for a meeting with the principal and the assistant chapter chairman (Mr. Gerewitz) to respond to it. She stated that she would not meet with the principal without having someone with her.

Recently Miss Newman was demonstrating exercises to her physical education class. This required separating her legs. Her panty hose were split along a seam, and she was not wearing underpants. The class and her assistants were in a stir. Instead of turning the class over to an assistant, se continued to demonstrate. When the next day, her supervisor suggested that she wear underpants, she flew into a rage and called her a "lousy bitch". She then went to a male teacher nearby, picked up her dress, and showed him that she was wearing underpants. She repeated this performance the next day with Mr. Arnesen, chapter chairman. A full period discussion was held among her, the chapter chairman, Mr. Rommer (formerly her chairman), and the principal. It became evident to me that she could not be reasoned with, and a note was sent to her (Exhibit B). She filed a grievance. In connection with this, the following events occurred. She scotch-taped the statement appearing in Exhibit C on to a table in the teacher's lounge. She brought the torn panty hose to the Step 2 hearing, and asked the assistant superintendent to note the position of the hole. She distributed mimeographed sheets (Exhibit D) in the teachers' cafeteria. She brought the panty hose to the teachers' Cafeteria to show her colleagues.

Subsequent to the Step 2 decision, she designated students for role-playing in one physical education class. One girl was to pretend to have cramps; another to be wearing pantyhose with a hole near the crotch. She interrogated the girls in the class where the original incident occurred, one line each day, as to their reactions to the incident. In the process, she dismissed them late.

Miss Newman is insistent upon the following of regulations by her fellow teachers and by students. When it is pointed out to her that she is inconsistent in regard to her own behavior, she explains this away with complete self-justification.

Miss Newman over-reacts to situations and appears unable to exercise self-control and reasoned judgment. Efforts at two-way discussions are unavailing; her response to written notes of record is to file grievances charging harassment and persecution. Generally speaking, she is rigid, hostile, and suspicious. She balloons molehills into mountains. Incidents which would be glossed over by most teachers are built into a cause by Miss Newman.

January 26, 1970

Dr. Lang never checked the charges made against me. Dr. Lang never investigated the allegations made by Mr. Gordon. He never contacted me at all. This letter was received and acted upon immediately with total acceptance of its contents. The teacher is assumed to be guilty, arbitrarily.

Dr. Lang ordered me to appear for a medical exam, less than two weeks later in February, 1970 simply because Mr. Gordon wrote this letter requesting it.

What did the U.F.T. do? Nothing! Charles Loiacono, a field representative, was assigned to accompany me to the exam. Eugene Kaufman, the U.F.T. house counsel, said I must submit to the exam. I was assured that if I did not go for the exam. I could be charged with insubordination. I resented being forced to go at all. Why did I have to go? Because Mr. Gordon wrote a phony, concocted letter based on hearsay, opinion and distortion. The union, through Vincent Speranza, the grievance department head, Vito de Leonardis, staff director, advised me that the Union would protect me and see that my contractual rights were upheld. Not yet knowing the truth about the U.F.T. and still trusting, I agreed to go for the medical exam.

So Charles Loiacono accompanied me to the Board of Education medical division office at 65 Court Street, where the physicians examined me, in February.

The first doctor, a brunette woman, (Dr. Barbara Wright) was perfunctory in her remarks and handling of me. I noticed Mr. Gordon's letter propped up on her desk, immediately. While she took my blood pressure, she asked me questions about Mr. Gordon's accusations in the letter. I told her that the whole letter was a lie and was written to discredit me because I refused to be intimidated. When she asked anything specific, as, "Why did you fail 75 students at one time, in a class of 90?" I said, quite firmly, that this incident happened four years prior in 1966, and that class register was 135 pupils, not 90, and that I had carefully documented the reasons for the failures. In fact, I pointed out the fact that I was commended on my careful record-keeping in that class by my department chairman, Bob Rommer, and that he agreed with my marking of those students. This woman doctor made no comment, and continued her physical examination of me, in a detached manner. When she was finished, she ushered me to the large waiting room, and instructed me to sit there and wait to be called by a second doctor.

Mr. Loiacono told me that two doctors usually examine the teacher and that so far as he could tell, all went well.

We sat there about fifteen minutes, when we were approached by a middle-aged, stocky man who motioned us to follow him to his cubicle. He was the second doctor, and also was very mechanical in his attention to me. (Dr. Mark Wallfield)

"Miss Newman, you are a very attractive woman, and don't look your age," he began, looking at me, directly, to see my response to this complimentary remark. "I see that Dr. Wright has found you quite healthy, my dear, and except for a little albumen in your urine, there's nothing wrong at all. Can you explain it?"

"Thank you for the compliment, but you're the doctor. "I answered. "What does albumen mean?"

"Well, when did you have your period?" he queried.

"Just completed it yesterday," I replied.

"Well, that accounts for it, no doubt," he mused, looking over the folder in front of him, and then looking at me, intently. Then I realized he also had a copy of Mr. Gordon's letter and was consulting it, too, while looking me over.

He cleared his throat, and a weak smile appeared as he said, "Well, I certainly hope your problems with your principal are resolved at the U.F.T. office," while I continued on, homeward bound. Charlie assured me that the Union would let me know the results of my exams, as soon as they were forwarded. He urged me to try not to get upset at school, and to avoid contact with Mr. Gordon and Mrs. Ashepa.

To this day, I feel that Charles Loiacono was very sincere in his efforts as my field representative, and really tried to help me, a U.F.T. teacher who was maligned and abused by an unscrupulous weakling of a principal, and who had appealed to the Union for relief and protection.

To this day, I exclude Charles Loiacono and Mrs. Gladys Roth, the second field representative to whom I was assigned, after Charlie's departure from the Union, from any blame or responsibility for this nightmare, I do not believe that these two were aware of the corruption and betrayal of individual teachers by the Union. I believe that they tried to do an honest job, but were hampered and paralyzed by the Union's decision not to fight for individual teachers, but to just ignore them, and allow the Board of Education to destroy them, through phony hearing by phony hearing, violation by violation, without interference.

You can reach your own conclusions as you read on.

While I went about my daily tasks of teaching, preparing lesson plans, and coaching my bowling club girls, I was waiting for the results of my medical exams. I was waiting for a letter or phone call, which never came.

Chapter Nine

These Students are still Tenants In My File

THESE STUDENTS ARE STILL IN MY PROFESSIONAL FILE

In this chapter you'll meet three of those students whose letters of complaint were solicited by Mrs. Mildred Ashepa, the acting chairman of my department, for the principal. My response to each of them will also be presented.

According to the teachers' contract, a teacher must see and sign a paper that he or she has read the letter. Then the teacher's letter of reply must be affixed to the original letter, so that both sides of the complaint are available.

Eileen Schulman was a very pretty, blonde teenager, with long hair and fair skin. Lovely to look at, but that's where it ends. Her classroom manner was harsh, and belligerent. She chattered constantly, in the class, while I was teaching, and while other students were answering questions or participating in open discussions. She was very rude, and I asked her many times to raise her hand when she wanted to say something, but she continued to call out and interrupt, whenever she wished to participate.

I warned Eileen several times during those first 6 weeks, to modify her behavior and to stop her incessant chattering to her neighbors, or I would fail her in citizenship at the first marking period.

Do you like sitting next to someone who constantly talks during a movie? Haven't you ever asked someone seated next to you, or nearby, to keep quiet so you could hear what the actors were saying on the stage? Well, Eileen is that kind of student and I, as her teacher, attempted to show her the better way.

She had ample opportunity to improve her attitude, and since she ignored my requests and continued her interruptions, I gave her the Unsatisfactory rating in citizenship, that she had earned.

Report cards were distributed on Friday, March 20th, to all students. Eileen was in my class that day. No hint or word came from her to me, about what was to follow. This is the letter she wrote, on March 20th, 1970:

"To Whom it may concern: March 20, 1970.

I am writing this letter as a result of actions by Miss Newman. I have been in her class for the past two months. The following conversation involving the topic First Aid made me write the letter.

"Miss Newman, A lady once slipped on the ice and my friend and I helped her up, only to have her say to us, "get away, you hippies". Miss Newman then replied to me, "She probably thought you were a dope addict or some sort of tramp."

I was embarrassed and hurt by this. Since then she ahs been picking on me and accusing me of having an "attitude of revolt" towards her. To explain, if I have different ideas than these of Miss Newman's, I'm revolting against her.

She gave me a U in citizenship and I feel the only way I can continue is if I am transferred out of her class. My mother was very angry and threatened to go to more drastic measures to deal with Miss Newman but I told her I could solve it by just getting out of her class.

I have spoken to Mrs. Ashepa and she will admit me to her class of Hygiene same period.

Yours truly,

Eileen Schulman

6-26

I found this letter in my mailbox, in the teachers' workroom, at 3:30 p.m. as I was leaving the building. It was attached to a note from Mr. Gordon shown below:

Office of the Principal
To: Miss Newman

Subject: I have received the accompanying note from
one of your students. I am transmitting a copy to you in
order to give you an opportunity to react to the statements
made. On the basis of the statements in the note, I shall
honor the change of class request, unless your reply should
indicate otherwise.

David Gordon
Principal

Here is my official response, to Eileen Schulman's letter, which I
handed in to Mr. Gordon's secretary, on April 17, 1970, more than
three weeks after the complaint. It is important that you, the reader,
realize that I tried to talk to Mr. Gordon about Eileen, and found him
to be unbelievably unreachable.

Bob Arnesen, the chapter chairman, tried to talk to him and got
nowhere. At the Step One hearing, in which I charged the principal
with unfair and inequitable treatment of me, Bob tried to determine
why Mr. Gordon had honored Eileen's statements in arbitrary fashion,
without first asking for Miss Newman's reasons for giving Eileen the
Unsatisfactory rating.

The principal's set jaw and totally closed expression showed us
that there was no point, whatsoever, to continue the grievance
hearing, since we were literally talking to ourselves. We left the
office, and I knew, in my heart, that there was no point to Step One
hearings at all. This was my third one, and in each one, the accused
was also the judge. Does the enormity of the whole hopeless, farce
reach you? If not, then I must find other ways to impress you with the
grievant's position, one of utter futility.

April 13, 1970

Dear Mr. Gordon:
Re: This is my response to the Eileen Schulman letter.

I have asked the girl, on several occasions, to stop calling out when she wishes to participate. I have asked her and all the other girls, <u>not to gab</u> during our film <u>sessions,</u> and Eileen has chatted away. She is very aggressive and rude, when she does answer a question.

When I've done visual aids, medical magazine ads, health department literature, etc. and attempted to discuss the narcotics problem, Eileen lashed out with "What do these doctors know, anyhow? They only work on guinea pigs. They don't know everything." Her manner was unacceptable, and I suggested to her that she try to realize that there is a more gracious way to make classroom contributions. Discussion, not warfare, is the aim.

I was teaching first aid in a very professional manner and all my remarks were appropriate and valid. A teacher is not a mind-reader. A teacher presents information, visual aids, outside agencies' literature, shows films, etc., etc. in order to do a top job. If a child says, three weeks later, that something the teacher said in an explanation hurt her feelings, it is not valid. Eileen got the U in citizenship because she deserved it.

Her inability to face up to her own behavior, (rude calling out in class, constant chattering) is <u>her problem, her responsibility, not mine</u>. My responsibility is to make the classroom lessons interesting, dynamic, life-connected, so as to get the students involved in their own health problems, and the community's and thereby become healthier young adults.

Your honoring her complaint, and Mrs. Ashepa's promising to take her into her class, is indefensible and professionally destructive to teacher effectiveness. You did not offer me, the teacher involved, the very basic courtesy, a chance to be heard. Did you hear my side of the story before I filed a Step One grievance? No! Did you ascertain from me what the facts, as I see them, are, in this matter? No. Did you try to find out Eileen's part in the earning of a U? No. Did you ask me anything? No, you did not. You Xeroxed the letter, made arrangements with Mrs. Ashepa to transfer the girl out of my Hygiene class into hers, totally on the basis of what Eileen said, unverified, uninvestigated, unproven, and unanswered by me.

    Utterly indefensible!

                  Sincerely,

                  Francine H. Newman
                  Health Education Department

One more factor regarding this particular case must be mentioned here.

I asked the chapter chairman to search out the reason why Eileen had written this letter. He spoke to the school psychologist, Lester Marks, who informed Bob that Eileen had been coming in to his office, for psychological counseling. She had problems with her mother. From what he had learned, it was apparent that Eileen feared her mother and it was easy to guess that she was afraid to tell her mother about the "U" in citizenship from me, so she sought a way to evade facing up to her own poor behavior, and with Mrs. Ashepa's help, she wrote the letter, thereby getting herself off the hook, by denouncing the teacher, and supplying Mrs. Ashepa with more manufactured evidence for the impending U rating that was being arranged for me, by Mr. Gordon.

Rona Brief was a student in Mrs. Ashepa's gym class, where I was assisting teacher. A major part of my responsibility as the number two teacher was supervising the locker room at the beginning and end of the period. Keeping order and helping students with any problems that may have occurred with a locker or missing sneaker or gym suit or whatever, was my main task. I generally led the class up to the locker room at the end of the class session, and then remained at the door, to prevent students form leaving the locker room before the dismissal bell rang.

Rona was coming up the stairs alongside of me on this day, and suddenly she blurted out, in her smart-aleck manner, "Hey, Miss Newman, how come you never gave us as much time to change as Mrs. Ashepa does?" She ran past me as I answered her that if she thought Mrs. Ashepa was perfect, it was fine with me. Then, from her locker area, she shouted back, "Mrs. Ashepa sure is better than you will ever be." I was taken aback at her rudeness, but it was nothing new to me. I had met Rona before, several terms earlier, and regarded her as a very sullen, nasty girl. I called out to Rona that her remarks were unacceptable and rude and that she was going to have to see the dean.

Her answer to me typifies her manner. It's a shame that her parents had allowed her behavior to get so out-of-control, and had not come in to see to it that Rona was helped and disciplined. Instead, as I had seen last term, she ran off at the mouth and said whatever she felt like saying to a teacher. I feel that it is wrong to allow a student to speak to me that way, and I believe in making the student responsible for her own actions.

Her actual answer was, "Go ahead and see how far it gets you."

Mrs. Ashepa was coming up the locker room stairs at this moment, and I related the incident to her, and asked that she speak to Rona about her nastiness to me.

Nothing further was ever said about the incident, and I assumed that the chairman was going to discipline Rona.

I sent a note to Rona's grade adviser, Mrs. Helen Arum, about Rona's behavior, and asked her to speak to her, too.

Just before the marking period ended, I spoke to Rona's home room teacher, Mrs. Hopp, and asked her to place a "U" rating on a blank line on the report card with the words, Miss Newman, Health Education #2 teacher, next to it, so that my remark would be in addition to the Health Education #1 teacher, Mrs. Ashepa's grade. Cafeteria teacher, librarians, and deans could give citizenship marks on the report cards, too, so that every teacher with whom a student came into contact, could be represented on the card.

Mrs. Hopp asked me to write her a note to remind her that she should put my mark in, and she commiserated with me that Rona was a very troublesome student, indeed, and I asked her if she was giving her an unsatisfactory citizenship mark, too. No comment came forth at this question.

Mr. Sage, a social studies teacher who had heard me talking about Rona in the lounge, also volunteered the comment that he had taught Rona and found her to be rude, an aggressive girl. When I asked him what kind of mark he was giving her, he did not give me a direct answer, but said, rather, that he had not decided yet.

So, although Rona's outburst occurred on March 5th, and the report cards were given out on March 20th, I was not officially informed by Mr. Gordon that he was placing letters in my file about the Rona Brief matter, and the Estella Pino letter and the Maria Feldman letter, until April 7, 1970.

This illustrates the devious and unfair technique used by Mr. Gordon, in his attempts to stack my file with these solicited letters. He repeatedly notifies the teacher, me, weeks after he has already arbitrarily believed and honored the student's complaint, so that the denial of due process, of allowing an accused person to face the accuser, was perpetrated against me, over and over again.

Here is Rona Brief's complaint letter:

3/5/70

Dear Mrs. Ashepa:

This letter is in reference to what happened 5th period in the locker room. The kids, me, and Miss Newman were going up to change so I asked her a question. I said "How come you never gave us as much time to change as Mrs. Ashepa does?" (I once had her as a head)

So Miss Newman said, "Well, if Mrs. Ashepa's perfect...(she didn't say anything after that) So I said "she (Mrs. Ashepa) sure is better than you are, and better than you will ever be." She didn't say anything then. After a short while, she said she would give me a salmon. So I said "go ahead and see how far it gets you." Then you came up to the locker and called me. This is the truth, because my friends heard her, too.

Rona Brief
6 – 2

Here is my response to this letter, which I wrote on April 13, 1970:

Dear Mr. Gordon:
Re: Rona Brief case

It is Rona Brief who should be disciplined, corrected, helped, censured, for her nasty remarks to me in the girls' locker room. I reported her to Mrs. Ashepa, immediately, right in the locker room. Since Mrs. Ashepa did not give Rona the U for the first third, I gave my own U as an assisting teacher, in a separate box on the report card; alongside, not instead of, her teacher.

I am up in the locker room <u>3</u> periods each day, and there is a great deal of noise, movement, in a tense, rushed atmosphere. I see many infractions every day and only act on the most flagrant ones (cursing, sneaking out, nasty remarks).

Rona's letter should have been read, and then her mother should have been given a check sheet, and been asked to apologize for her actions.

No self-respecting teacher accepts verbal insults, to iron out, the student's difficulty.

To make a judgment on the basis of her statements, to not immediately upon reading Rona's letter, censure her for her snottiness, is using very poor judgment, and tends to undermine the teacher's effectiveness.

Your actions towards me, in this and in every other letter answered today, are nasty, one-sided, unprofessional, and constitute harassment of me.

Sincerely,
Francine H. Newman
Health Education Teacher

And now you shall read a letter of complaint from a student named Estella Pino. This letter is dated March 25, 1970, and apparently was written right after the report cards went out, on March 20th. My only comments before you read the letter are in the form of 4 probing questions:

-Would a principal use such an infantile whine of a letter to use as a letter of evidence against a teacher who has had an excellent teaching record for more than 20 years?
-Were the charges made investigated?
-Was the teacher called in to present her side of the complaint?
-Was the teacher informed of the complaint, before the student's charges were automatically accepted and honored?

You know the answers to these questions, but if there is a vestige of doubt remaining, here is Estella's letter:

March 25, 1970

To Whom It May Concern:

I would like to become a gym teacher. And I would like to get my class changed because I don't get along with Mrs. Newman. The reason is I misunderstood her and she gave me a zero. I don't think I was right because she is here to teach if we do anything wrong not to scold us; to help us if we need her.

I am also captain of my volleyball team. The girls elected me captain. She did not want me to be captain and refused to allow me to continue.

Everyone in the class complains but they are afraid. Yesterday she gave one girl seven zeroes in one period because she would not sit on her new dress. (Joyce Flood)

I brought my mother to school to see if I could get a change of class.

Estella Pino
Mrs. Gladys Pino

Here is my official response to this letter:

April 13, 1970

Dear Mr. Gordon:

Estella Pino's letter, which was Xeroxed and placed in my letterbox, without my <u>ever being made aware of its existence at all</u>, is the letter from a disruptive, bullying, unco-operative, hostile girl. She is a bully.

She does not respond to classroom instructions. She has a history from last term, and I'm sure, from junior high, of being a trouble-making, disruptive youngster.

When, one day, I removed her from the volleyball game, she poured out a stream of hate which must have been storing up for a long time, for about five minutes straight, and much of what she said was about herself and her picture of herself. ("Whaddya think? I'm some kind of animal, or something"), etc., etc., etc.

I asked my assisting teacher (Mrs. Jacobs) to escort her to the dean's office but she returned shortly because there was no dean on duty (Period 10) and the girl got dressed and went on her way. I noted it in my book.

Recently, I had a very small group of girls in front of me, and I decided to review all the square dance steps which had been danced over and over in the previous two weeks of coed square dancing, and to give the girls in front of me (about 32) instead of the whole class (about 65) a chance to earn <u>extra credit, extra good work marks, that day</u>. I <u>allemande left first</u>, because it always seems to be the one that is confusing because dancer must dance with person <u>other than the partner</u>. I went over it slowly, without the music, with the music, one group at a time, all groups together; about six times. I asked if everyone was ready because I felt ready to award plusses.

Estella did everything wrong. She gave her partner the wrong hand. She did nothing right! When I gave out credit to the girls deserving it, she launched into a tirade of venom. "You can't teach," etc.

Her letter is the work of a child who cannot reason, who cannot learn, who has long needed expert help, and who, when she is not allowed her way, attacks whoever may be there. She is an ambulatory temper-tantrum, looking for a place to explode. Her letter is invalid, is insulting to me and distortions abound. You accept her judgment, arbitrarily.

Your acceptance of this letter, your honoring her request for changing her class based on what she says, a girl who was a disrupter last term (Mrs. Leys' class) and has a long history of being unco-operative, unstable, (the two medically excused girls at my desk said, "She's at it again. She did the same thing last term in Mrs. Leys' class").

Your accepting her word, is professionally indefensible, and completely unwarranted. Two sides should be heard in every incident, before any decision is made. A teacher is a target and vulnerable up there at the front of a class, and the teacher's side of anything which affects or involves him or her should be heard, before any actions are taken by a principal.

Sincerely,

Francine H. Newman
Health Education Teacher

I was so disgusted by this time, that I did little more than file the letters away and tell the chapter chairman about the latest one. I kept asking him to set up another chapter meeting so that every faculty member would know exactly what was going on, but didn't have much hope that the teachers would do anything, because they had done nothing since the January meeting.

I was becoming numb, emotionally, as these slings and arrows of outrageous fortune kept being aimed at me. It was the most difficult term of my entire teaching career, but I knew that I had done nothing wrong, and in fact, was following all the school directives, all the Gordon policies on dealing with excessive lateness, cutting, excessive absenteeism, and disruptive behavior, and was being attacked by the principal, himself, because he was such a weakling.

Let me introduce you to four more tenants Mr. Gordon arranged housing for, in my professional file.

Believe it or not, one of them, a parent, is someone I've never met, seen, spoken to, phoned, received any message from, at any time, whatsoever. She is a total stranger, and yet Mr. Gordon arranged for her to write a letter of complaint about me, and placed it in my file as damaging evidence against me. Can you believe this? Please turn the page and try.

Chapter Ten

Formula For Destruction
Two Mothers Plus Two Daughters =
An unsatisfactory Rating For The
Teacher

FORMULA FOR DESTRUCTION: 2 MOTHERS AND 2 DISRUPTIVE DAUGHTERS = AN UNSATISFACTORY RATING FOR THE TEACHER

Open School Week is a familiar, nation-wide phenomena. Parents and relatives are invited to the schools to see their children's teachers.

Frequently, the student's art work or musical accomplishments are seen and heard at a special assembly or tea or other appropriate social ceremony. The principal is often more visible at this time than any other time, and is seen greeting parents, and giving the impression that all is well, and that the administration is delighted to see the parents.

At Far Rockaway High School, subject teachers are assigned to a classroom and the parents come in and see the teacher and ask all the questions they've prepared. If the teacher has a large group waiting, parents may have to be satisfied with a five minute or ten minute conference.

In the health education department, however, things are done a little differently. All the women health education teachers sit together in one classroom, Room 106, which is located in the same corridor as the gymnasium. The men gym teachers also share the same classroom arrangement, a few doors down. This arrangement has generally worked out fairly well.

A student hostess stands at the door and directs parents to the teacher they have come to see; if one teacher has a large number of parents, she gives them a number, and they are interviewed, in sequential order, and most of the parent conferences turn out pretty satisfactorily.

However, the appearance of a mother, Mrs. Wolf Feldman, in the doorway of Room 106, on March 23, 1970, was a horrible exception to the general goings-on at these open school week visitations.

I was seated at the front of the classroom. The other members of my department were scattered about the room, towards the rear, and were conversing quietly, among themselves, while waiting for their students' parents to arrive. The acting Chairman, Mrs. Ashepa, was also seated in the room, behind me, at the rear of the classroom.

Mrs. Feldman was the first mother to appear, asking to see me. She was accompanied by her daughter, Marla, one of my sophomore students. As she came towards me, I motioned her and Marla to seats nearby and urged them to make themselves comfortable.

I welcomed Mrs. Feldman and said that I was always glad to meet my students' parents. She said she had come for one reason and that was to find out why I had failed Marla in citizenship. I explained to her that Marla behaved very immaturely in gym; that she would walk off the volleyball court in the middle of a game, just because she felt like it. I added that Marla called out whatever was on her mind at a given moment, and that I had asked her to raise her hand and wait for me to acknowledge her. With more than a hundred girls in front of me, moving about, it was necessary to maintain discipline, for safety's sake.

Marla just sat there, and after hearing me, Mrs. Feldman turned to her daughter, who was wearing sunglasses, as usual. I was always asking Marla to remove her glasses, as they are a safety hazard in contact sport situation, and she always gave me an argument about how her mother allows her to wear them, and I tried to make the girl understand that I was responsible for whatever happened in the gym. Finally, she brought in a permission note from her mother, in which the mother assumed full responsibility for any accident that might occur. This was a kind of compromise which our department had worked out, for those students who refused to wear safety goggles we provided, or to remove their own glasses. I never really approved of this arrangement, but did co-operate fully in its use.

"Marla dear, you heard Miss Newman just now. What do you have to say about her answer?", the woman asked, in a very firm tone.

"Mommy, she's lying. She's always picking on me for wearing my glasses and chewing my aspergum, and it's not fair," Marla whined back.

"There you are, Miss Newman," sneered Mrs. Feldman. "I believe my daughter."

I attempted to object to Marla's petulant answer, which was a childish attempt to avoid facing the consequences of her immature behavior, but the mother suddenly stood up, and started yelling at me.

"Just a minute, Mrs. Feldman, I said. "Hold your horses. I'm sorry you choose to believe your daughter, because it shows me that you are encouraging her to continue to act in this babyish manner. I spoke to Marla many times during the past six weeks and if she made any attempt to co-operate, I would not have failed her in citizenship, but believe me, she deserves this mark."

"I'm not interested in your insulting remarks, Miss Newman," she lashed back, with her large frame drawn up to its full imposing height. "I'm leaving."

"Wait a minute, please," I said, in exasperation. "I want to run upstairs for a moment, and bring Mr. Arnesen, the chapter chairman down here, to hear your complaint. It's very important to me that he know what has gone on here."

"I'm not interested in this man," Mrs. Feldman fumed back. "Who is he? What has he got to do with my Marla?"

"I'm involved in a grievance procedure, and it is very important to me that Mr. Arnesen hear my side of what has gone on here, tonight. Please wait a moment. I'll be back in a minute," I explained, hastily, as I ran out the door.

Mrs. Feldman and Marla remained in the room, with all the members of my department sitting there. They had all witnessed the entire unpleasant scene. I was not present so I cannot write here what actually transpired, during the three or four minutes that I was out of the room. But here is what happened thereafter.

Bob came down with me, and Mrs. Feldman immediately began complaining to him about me. She also berated him for butting in, as she said, very heatedly, that I was a terrible teacher and she wasn't going to stand for it.

Bob tried, very weakly, to calm Mrs. Feldman down. He attempted to explain to her that there was no point in her yelling, as she was disturbing everyone else. While I stood there, helplessly, Mrs. Ashepa came to the front of the room, and put her arms around Mrs. Feldman's shoulder and emitted a statement which I shall never forget. "You see, Mr. Arnesen, this is another disgusting exhibition on the part of Miss Newman."

I stood there, aghast, nonplussed, unable to move.

Then Mrs. Ashepa turned toward the other gym teachers in the room, and they began praising Marla and reassuring Mrs. Feldman that Marla was a lovely girl and they had never had any trouble with her.

Mrs. Helen Arum said that Marla had been in her class last year and was no trouble at all.

Mrs. Dorris Silverman, the swimming teacher, extolled the virtues of Marla while in her swimming class.

After this, Mrs. Ashepa escorted Mrs. Feldman and Marla out of the room and down the corridor. Bob said his usual, "Take it easy, Fran" and ran upstairs to his waiting parents, while I stood there, rooted to the floor, by the disgust and hopelessness that engulfed me.

I had two choices as to how to spend the next hour and a half.

I could either just sit in the front of the room, with the teachers, or I could move my things out into the hall, and sit in the corridor, and greet any other parents there. I chose the latter path, and spent the remaining time outside my assigned classroom. A few parents stopped by to greet me and say that their daughters had instructed them to go and meet Miss Newman, since they liked me. This was a nice balancing experience, and did help somewhat to assuage the anger and despair I was feeling this particular night. When the gong sounded, and the session was over, I quickly picked up my coat from my locker and dashed out of the school to my car. I drove directly home, and went to bed, hoping to forget all that had happened.

I noticed that Marla was not in class the next two days, March 24 and 25, 1970.

On Thursday, March 26, 1970, I found a note in my letter box, signed by the principal's secretary, Miss Frant, indicating that Marla was now assigned to Mr. Gordon's office, in lieu of attending gym class, as a clerical assistant, and attached to it was a doctor's note.

The doctor's note was signed by Emanuel Levokove, M.D., of 2247 Mott Avenue, Far Rockaway, and asked that Marla be excused from gym for the balance of the term. Now, under ordinary conditions, this would be fine. But we see here a deceptive, calculated attempt to provide an excuse for Marla to be removed from my class. You see, dear reader, the doctor's note was addressed to the principal, not to me, the gym teacher, or the health education chairman, and this was the first time in all my twenty-five years of teaching that an excuse note from gym was addressed to a principal.

I could see how phony and unethical all this was. After all, Marla had been playing volleyball and actively participating in square dancing, for the whole first third of the term and there had been no note about any kind of strain, pain or whatever. And then, suddenly, right after her mother's visit, she is removed from my class, and a phony excuse note is hastily provided, from Dr. Levokove, who must bear responsibility for his part in this outrageous fraud.

I decided to investigate the matter, further, by dropping in at Dr. Levokove's office, and asking him how the note came to be written, at this particular time. I intended to explain to him that I was a doctor's daughter, and had asked my dad what he thought of the suddenness of the medical excuse, and he said by all means visit Dr. Levokove and ask him, personally, and then I would know the actual facts in the matter.

On Friday afternoon, March 27, 1970, I stopped at Dr. Levokove's home, and rang the bell. The doctor's wife and son were there, but the doctor wasn't. Mrs. Levokove was very cordial, and invited me in, and I told her why I was there. Her son, a young man I judged to be in his early twenties, was unpacking some groceries and was listening, intently, to our conversation.

The doctor's wife said that if I cared to leave my phone number, she'd have the doctor call me back. She then added that her husband was a busy man, and in case he forgot or was unable to call me back, I could call him at Peninsula General Hospital. I told her I appreciated her cordiality, thanked her appropriately, and drove home. Fully expecting the doctor to call that evening, I stayed home, even though it was the beginning of the Easter vacation, and I would have preferred to have gone out to dinner with a friend, to celebrate a week's respite from a most unpleasant and difficult school atmosphere.

The doctor did not call me back that evening.

On Monday morning, I called Peninsula General Hospital, and asked to speak to Dr. Levokove. He was reached by the operator, and asked who was calling. When I identified myself, Dr. Levokove immediately said, in a very curt manner, "Miss Newman, I don't want to talk to you," and hung up. Wasn't that nice, friendly gesture from a local neighborhood physician? I could only conclude from this that my suspicion that the note was a phony one, to cover Mr. Gordon's collusion with Mrs. Feldman, to get Marla out of gym, which is a required subject for a New York State diploma, was correct, and that my nightmare was growing more and more involved every minute.

Interestingly enough, when I tried to discuss this with Bob Arnesen, Abe Gerewitz, Maxwell Cohen, they tried to make light of this, and urged me to calm down, keep cool, and not get upset. This seemingly friendly attempt on their part was really a desire to protect themselves. All subsequent events show this to be the real reason behind their false concern.

The following letters were placed in my letterbox, after April 7th. The date is significant, because 2 full weeks had elapsed before I was officially apprised of Mrs. Feldman's letter. Her letter, dated March 23, 1970, was obviously written on Open School night, when she came up to complain.

March 23, 1970

Marla Feldman

My daughter has been upset with her gym teacher since the beginning of this term and what brought it to a head was on particular incident which prompted the teacher to giver Marla a "U" on her report card, which I feel is not quite right for a gym mark. She has been doing well all along in gym and loves it.

I came to see the teacher on Open School Day (Miss Francine Newman) and she accused my child of being rude, of being a liar, of being insolent and not brought up right! The incident that I refer to was that Marla was chewing gum in class. She was given permission to do this the week before because of a medical problem (diet).

Miss Newman said that Marla opened up a big mouth to her when she told Marla to spit out the gum and Marla tried to explain and she would not listen. When Marla came home, she told me the story exactly as it happened, and of course I believed her because Marla is not one to lie. She came home very upset.

When I tried to see Miss Newman today she would not listen to Marla's story, and she would not listen to me either. She just insisted that Marla was a liar, and was not brought up right and was very insolent.

She always insists that Marla take off her glasses. Marla cannot see without her glasses and she brought a note to that effect. She still insists that Marla take off her glasses. She is constantly picking on her and every day when Marla comes home I hear the same story. I am not going to let any teacher make a nervous wreck out of my child – especially in gym.

It is not a major subject and a class she has always liked and enjoyed.

When I came in and started to speak to her and told her what I came about – before I got halfway through, she said just wait a minute I will be back. She went to get someone – she came back and said who are we waiting for – she said a man I want to listen to this – was he in the gym class when this was taking place? She said it is something to do with a suit pending and she wanted this man to listen in to the conversation. I said I don't want to be involved in your suits. This is between you and my child and me. I am sorry I am not waiting for this man. I have other teachers to see and I am leaving.

As I was leaving, the man, in question, arrived and Miss Newman repeated the same uncomplimentary remarks about my daughter.

Mrs. Wolf Feldman

I wrote my answer to this letter and handed it Mr. Gordon's secretary, who with her usual averted gaze, mumbled that she would give it to him.

April 13, 1970

Dear Mr. Gordon:

Re: This is my response to the <u>Marla Feldman</u> letter, written by her mother, Mrs. Wolf Feldman.

It is a complete distortion of the incident, Mrs. Feldman attacked me verbally and started yelling at me after:

1)I had welcomed her and said I'm always glad to meet the mothers. She sat down, Marla sat down and I was seated.
2)I explained that Marla had been rude, insolent and, in my opinion, <u>immature,</u> and deserving of the U in citizenship.

She then said, "Well, that's your side of the story. Let's hear Marla's."

I said, "fine."

Marla, sitting right there, said "Miss Newman's lying. I wasn't insolent to her at all."

I then said, "Mrs. Feldman, you've heard my story. I asked Marla to stop chewing the gum, and she emitted a torrent of heated words. "If my throat gets dried out, it'll be your fault, Miss Newman," etc.

Mrs. Feldman then stood up and started <u>yelling at me,</u> Mr. Gordon.

"My daughter always tells the truth. My daughter Marla would never lie. There must be something wrong with you," etc.

I said, "Mrs. Feldman, please wait a minute. There's a gentleman upstairs who I'd like to hear what you say. I'll be right back."

I got Mr. Arnesen to come down for a minute, <u>after the private interview</u> became <u>less private,</u> because <u>Mrs. Feldman began shouting at me.</u>

When I returned, Mrs. Feldman began yelling to Mr. Arnesen in the same fashion that I, Miss Newman, am a terrible teacher and that Marla is a perfect child – she always tells the truth.

At this point, Mrs. Mildred Ashepa, <u>said,</u> in front of <u>Mrs. Feldman</u> and <u>Marla</u> and the whole <u>girl's health education department,</u> "This is a <u>disgusting</u> exhibition on the part of Miss Newman." She came forward, put her arm around the mother, and they left.

Mrs. Ashepa's remark is completely wrong, unwarranted, distinctly hostile and distorted. I take exception to this, since <u>no supervisor</u> should say <u>judgmental remarks</u> in front of a child, <u>ever.</u>

Your honoring of <u>Mrs. Ashepa's</u> and <u>Mrs. Feldman's remarks,</u> without hearing my side, is <u>absolutely</u> and <u>unequivocally indefensible.</u> Your one-sided, arbitrary rulings are contrary to all educational and legal traditions.

To remove Marla from my class, place her as a clerical aide in <u>your office,</u> is proof of the pudding.

Marla was busy playing volleyball, and square-dancing, as of <u>Monday, March 23,</u> and was busy lying to her mother and to me at this meeting on Tuesday, March 24, and then I get the <u>first doctor's</u> notice in <u>25 years addressed to the principal,</u> instead of the health education teacher or chairman or nurse or health counselor, excusing her for the whole term for a sprain?

The sequence of events speaks for itself.

Last, but not least, there is a departmental rule that <u>no child</u> may ever wear glasses during <u>contact sports,</u> unless the child brings a note from home or from a doctor, assuming full responsibility, in case of accident.

When the note is brought in, I honor it. We have safety goggles to give to the girls who wish to use them. We have a poster at the front of the gym. It's for the students' safety; for the protection of the <u>child's eyes</u>. Who would be sued? The teacher!

Yet, you honor Mrs. Feldman's complaint that I kept telling Marla to remove her glasses, too.

Ridiculous! Indefensible!

Sincerely,

Francine H. Newman
Health Education Department

I never saw Marla Feldman again. She received full credit for a term of health education, while sitting in Mr. Gordon's office as a messenger, protected by a phony doctor's note and an unethical principal.

The thought occurs to me here that there must be quite a few diplomas awarded, that are <u>unearned</u>. This might be an interesting subject for a doctoral thesis.

And then another student was removed from my class at the same time. Helen Sheridan, one of the most insolent and un-cooperative sophomores I have ever met, suddenly dropped out of my class, right after the marking period.

She just sat on her floor spot and smouldered. Helen's general facial expression was a sneer. Since she was unusually well-developed physically, and tall, she appeared confined rather than comfortable in her gym suit.

She was un-cooperative and unspontaneous. I spoke to her several times during class activities about her non-involvement. She just walked off the gym floor whenever she wanted to. I wrote her grade adviser and asked him to see her and encourage her to do some work and try to achieve in my class. He, Maxwell Cohen, wrote back that he had sent for her several times, but she failed to appear for any of the scheduled appointments.

I checked her permanent records to see what her attitudes and grades may have been in junior high school, and found that she had a confidential file from the feeding school, but, of course, the teacher who is trying to teach a student is not allowed to see the confidential file, but judging from Helen's immature petulance and lack of work, I can speculate that she had emotional difficulties of some sort which had not been resolved earlier, and they were still boiling inside her. Helen's eyes were strange – they blazed with unfriendliness and did not soften or dim while I talked to her after class. I had told her that I was giving her an unsatisfactory citizenship mark for the first marking period because of her actions and encouraged her to try harder, to do the work, and try to participate more, and that it was up to her what mark she earned.

This letter was placed in my letterbox by Mr. Gordon with his usual accompanying note, about having received a note from a Mrs. Sheridan, complaining about me, and would I be kind enough to let him know my side of all this.

This malicious game he was playing was all too apparent to me; what's the point of even bothering to ask me anything, days and weeks <u>after</u> he had <u>already arbitrarily, one-sidedly,</u> honored the mother's charges, placed her letter in my file, removed the student from my class and refused to keep the appointment to discuss the latest complaint, without even giving a reason. Here's the letter Helen Sheridan's mother sent in to Mrs. Ashepa:

> April 12, 1970
> 357 Bayside
> Roxbury, N.Y. 11697

Mrs. Ashepa
Chairman, Physical Education
Far Rockaway H.S.
Far Rockaway, N.Y.

Dear Mrs. Ashepa:

I have recently been in contact with Mr. Farrell in regard to a problem my daughter Helen has been having in her gym class. I am aware the difficulties have arisen from a misunderstanding and what has continued has been due to human emotional problems and I believe Helen, too, understands this but, the fact remains Helen has been told she can expect a failing term mark as a result.

Over a period of years, she has had difficulty at attaining passing grades and has been proud of recent ability to succeed and therefore finds it difficult to accept a failure based not on her ability to work but based on someone's inability to cope with her own personal problem.

It has greatly disturbed her emotional (her frame of mind, appetite, tears) and I feel that I must ask for your assistance.

I would very much appreciate it if her gym class could be changed and she be marked on the basis of her athletics and efforts in regards to her work.

Thank you for your kind attention to this matter and for the help you could extend to us.

> Yours truly,
> Mrs. Marjorie Sheridan
> GR 4-3895

As you read my reply to this letter, please be aware of the dates of both letters. Mrs. Sheridan wrote her letter on April 12, 1970 and I wrote my official reply on May 4, 1970. Why did I reply to such an obviously arranged letter more than three and a half weeks later? Because I was not apprised of the letter till after Mr. Gordon had already honored it and transferred Helen into Mrs. Arum's class, and although promising a discussion about Mrs. Sheridan's complaint, to the chapter chairman, he never held this meeting and so it was May 4th, and I wrote my official reply to this latest set-up.

> Monday, May 4, 1970

Dear Mr. Gordon

Re: Helen Sheridan's mother's letter.

Helen Sheridan is in my Health Education period 10 class. She is a nasty, uncooperative, belligerent girl. She has used abusive language to me. ("Go to hell"). She has walked off the gym floor during assigned activities.

She has been excessively unprepared. She has shown below the minimum effort. She has not brought in a required medical (due since junior high).

She was given an appointment for the school doctor but did not show up for it.

For all these reasons, she earned a "U" rating in citizenship for the first third in my class.

For you, Mr. Gordon, to honor her mother's nasty and unfounded claims in her letter, is wrong, unprofessional, and constitutes harassment and unfair treatment of me, a teacher who performs her tasks with professionalism and a high sense of responsibility.

For you to remove Helen Sheridan from my class without meeting me and Mr. Arnesen as we requested two weeks ago, is professionally indefensible since my rights of due process are being violated.

You have not observed me, you don't know what behavior was exhibited by a child in a class, and yet you one-sidedly honor the child's request, or the student's parent's request without hearing the teacher's side at all.

> Francine H. Newman
> Health Education Teacher

I am still reacting to the unfairness of Mrs. Sheridan's letter. It is still hard for me to realize that a woman who has never met me, who doesn't know me at all, can write such a letter.

My bitterness about these letters is still unresolved, because here it is 1970, and Mrs. Sheridan's letter is still sitting in my file, as part of accepted, unverified, unchecked proof that Mr. Gordon's "U" rating was well-founded.

This feeling within me of the injustice, the calculated malice of Mr. Gordon, Mrs. Ashepa, Superintendent (Wilner), the medical division personnel at 110 Livingston Street, has translated itself into a determination to expose them to public view.

It has also reinforced the title I've given to this chapter and its summary sentence which is when two guilt-ridden mothers of two troubled daughters look for a target person or a scapegoat, on which to hang their own inadequacies, and they find a principal like a Mr. Gordon, the combination of them all can fuse into a tightly-knit web of horror for the person unwilling to be their scapegoat.

Chapter Eleven

April and May 1990
The Worst is Yet to Come

APRIL AND MAY, 1970 – THE WORST IS YET TO COME

While the Feldman and Sheridan mothers were busy writing their phony letters, Mr. Gordon was setting up two more letters for my file, so that it was becoming stuffed full of complaints against me, thereby insuring the basis for the Unsatisfactory rating being readied for June.

I was awaiting a Step Two hearing at Superintendent Abraham Wilner's office, about the Eileen Schulman letter, and was also preparing to speak to the entire U.F.T. Chapter about the cramming of my file by the principal.

During the third week of April, 1970, when this meeting was held, all the teachers seemed very interested and concerned about what was being done to me by the principal. Everyone had been at the January meeting and knew what the principal was up to, then, too, but had done nothing, except issue a resolution against the principal's actions, and now, I was hoping for more from my colleagues.

After I spoke to the chapter, I left the room so that Bob and Abe, the two chairmen, could tie everything together. I did not want to witness the goings-on, but hoped that the staff would rally around me and decide to storm the principal's office, and demand that he cease his harassment of me.

"Fran," Abe had told me, "we're going to try to clean up this mess. Many of the staff have told me privately that they don't condone Mrs. Ashepa's actions, and they really feel very bad about what's happened."

"Really, Abe," I retorted, "How touching! How sweet! But what are they doing about it? Huh, Abe?"

He looked away, and didn't answer the question.

"Honest, Fran, we'll try hard to get the facts from your department," he went on, in his quiet, semi-apologetic manner, "I am hopeful that this kind of thing won't ever happen again."

"We'll see," I said. "Let me know as soon as you hold that meeting, Abe. I'll be interested. Thanks!"

"O.K., Fran. Meanwhile, please don't get upset. Take it easy," he advised, sympathetically. "You know I'm on your side." He left the lunchroom, and I followed a few minutes later.

Then some unusual things happened.

Some young addicts from the newly opened Odyssey House in Far Rockaway came to the high school, to speak to all the students. Instead of the usual assembly-type setting, my department was placed in charge of this program, and it was decided that all the gym classes would meet together, for rap sessions with these addicts. In addition, the teachers were asked to leave, and remain outside, so that the students would feel free to speak out, without fear of faculty disapproval or censure.

It seemed like a good idea, to me, as the Rockaway community had been against an Odyssey House being opened in its midst, and there was quite a furor for many weeks. This might be an excellent way to allay fears and stem drug use by our students, I felt, and was enthusiastic about the event.

While standing outside the boys' gym, I chatted with Ira May, a student government leader, about things in general, and as an outcome of this conversation, and something else I noticed, decided to invite some seniors out to lunch, as my guests, in the very near future. Ira made general comments about the difficulties in being a high school student at this point in time, and I said that teachers were having their problems, too.

It occurred to me that I knew a lot of fine, bright kids who were about to be graduated into challenges of the world outside, and I wanted to share with them the problems that I, one of their teachers, was faced with at the school. I decided to invite Elaine Soloway, a lovely, sensitive senior, who was captain of the girls' bowling club of which I was the faculty adviser, and Carol Silverman, a perky, witty girl, and Karen Hopenwasser, a brainy, introspective student with whom I had had serious chats about school life. She was editor of the school newspaper and had earned a Westinghouse scholarship, and had been one of the liveliest members of my hygiene class the term before.

In addition, to these three girls and Ira, I invited Lorraine Friedman, a very athletically inclined student who had shone with enthusiasm and spirit the previous semester, in my health education class, and one other girl name Toni Ferrara, who, like Lorraine, was extremely interested in sports and was involved in our various club programs in the department.

I sent letters to Ira, and Karen, and Carol, via their homeroom period, and personally invited Elaine and Lorraine when I saw them during the course of the next day's activities. Since Toni was not in one of my classes this term, I asked Lorraine to invite her, and she agreed to do so.

The luncheon was scheduled for Friday afternoon of the following week.

The "something else I noticed," which I referred to a few pages back, bears prominent mention here, because its occurrence let to further developments later in the month.

Since I was the assistant teacher in the gym during the ninth period each day, the fraudulent situation was taking place right before my eyes, and could not be unnoticed. Mrs. Helen Arum was the teacher of this sophomore gym class. It was her regularly assigned class, yet she allowed her extra-curricular volleyball club, to sit and watch her teach her own class every Wednesday afternoon. So what, you might correctly respond? What does that mean?

Well, the club was scheduled to meet for 2 hours, from 12:30 to 2:30, every Wednesday afternoon, at the Hartman "Y" across the street, yet for 45 minutes of their club session, Mrs. Arum was busy teaching her regular class, yet she was also being paid extra to conduct the volleyball club, after school, as a totally separate activity. The P.S.A.L. club activities must be conducted in 2 consecutive hours or the club may meet an hour before and an hour <u>after</u>, not during, the teacher's regular school day.

I had been coaching and supervising P.S.A.L. athletic clubs for almost 20 years, and knew the rules, and observed them.

The dishonesty of Mrs. Arum was glaringly apparent. Here she was, being paid extra for conducting a two-hour volleyball club, and the club girls were spending the ninth period, inactively, sitting on the gym platform, and along the wall.

The irony here is that Mrs. Arum willingly signed the department's letter to the U.F.T. maligning and excoriating me as a teacher, back in December, 1969, and here she is accepting paychecks for work she was not performing.

I thought this was quite interesting, and I went over to this teacher, a short, slim, self-effacing blonde, whose whispery voice and timid manner under the best circumstances in the gym, made her efficacy questionable, and asked her to explain to me how she could justify having her club sitting there, doing nothing, and taking money for it.

She didn't like the question one bit, and its directness caused her to wince. "Well, Miss Newman, when you look at it your way, I guess I am wrong," she whined. "But if I don't do it this way, then I wouldn't be able to have the club at all."

I looked at this teacher. She was busy stealing unearned money and justifying it by saying she couldn't have a club otherwise.

"Mrs. Arum, are you just accepting pay for one hour of coaching? Is that the story? If so, then of course, I'll apologize at once for making mention of this. Tell me, now, please, because I intend to report this to the P.S.A.L office, immediately," I said, firmly.

She blanched beneath her already pale complexion. "Mrs. Ashepa had given me permission to have the club and that's all I'm going to say on this matter." She turned and walked away from me.

So there it was! Mrs. Ashepa was aiding and abetting a fraud, too, and she was championed by the principal. She solicited phony letters saying all kinds of things about me (these came from the kids) and now she's helping to make phony extra-curricular club activities payroll. I wasn't surprise. I could only sigh in deep despair, and seek Bob Arnesen or Abe Gerewitz's attention to this newest link in the chain of deceit and smear that was being forged by some very unscrupulous people.

I went to the pay phones and they were occupied, so dashed back to the extension phone in the girl's emergency room, and made my call to the P.S.A.L. headquarters. I reached the woman in charge, Miss Wigiser, and told her all about Mrs. Arum and the volleyball club and answered her questions on this startling piece of information. She mused, momentarily, with me about the current low register of my bowling club, as a diverting tactic to draw attention away from the main purpose of my call, which may have upset her. She thanked me for calling in a very perfunctory manner, and suggested that I have Mrs. Ashepa call her, and this I refused to do. "Well, Fran, I'll probably see Mildred this afternoon at a Games Committee meeting anyway, and I'll discuss this with her then," was her closing remark.

Typically, when I broached the news of what I had just discovered to Bob, he played it down and said wasn't there enough trouble already!

"Yes, of course, Helen Arum's wrong," he agreed, "but let's not make a big fuss about this. I'll speak to the boss and to Mildred Ashepa and try to straighten things out, but I just can't afford to spend so much time on you, Fran. You're wearing me out. I really feel you're making unfair inroads into my time."

I looked at him and shuddered. I'm being attacked from all sides, unfairly, and now I discover that one of my attacker's is stealing money from the P.S.A.L., and my chapter chairman is worried that he is spending too much time on my real problems. I was very hurt by his insensitivity, but I didn't show it, directly.

"You're supposed to be protecting me, Bob, as the union person in the school. If Gordon is harassing me and stuffing my file, and I find out that Helen Arum is stealing, what the hell do you want from me! I'm the victim, not the perpetrator."

Bob looked a little sheepish, but I wasn't fooled by this. He had just revealed himself. The mask was off and I realized that my U.F.T. chapter chairman was interested in his own welfare, not mine.

"I'm sorry, Fran. Forget what I said," he suggested.

"Sure, Bob, sure," I lied back, choking on the realization of how terribly unfair his attitude was.

"I know you're a busy guy, but when you accept the job of chapter chairman, you've got to go all out for the teacher. Otherwise, who the hell needs a chapter chairman or a staff relations committee? There'd be no point to having a union or anything like it, right? So long, now. See you around."

Bob looked pained as I walked away from him, but his discomfort was due to his own timidity, rather than anything I said. He was obviously getting batted around by the principal, but then, so was I, and Bob was supposed to protect me from Mr. Gordon. Mr. Gordon was busy violating the contract and harassing a U.F.T. teacher unmercifully and Bob was supposed to try to improve the situation. And, of course, Abe Gerewitz, his co-chairman, was supposed to share the obviously onerous burden of protecting any U.F.T. member from unfair administrative tactics.

I decided to make a significant gesture of appreciation to Abe and Bob, for all the time they were "wasting" on me. And since Bob actually said that my problems were taking away time he should be spending at home with his family, theatre tickets for the two couples seemed like the right choice. I bought four orchestra seats for a Saturday evening performance, figuring that Bob and Abe and their wives would have dinner before the show and thereby spend a lovely evening on the town.

Both men protested vigorously that I should not have done this and there was no need to spend all that money on expensive tickets as they were only too glad to help me and they empathized with the nightmare, etc., etc., but I convinced them that it was only a gesture of goodwill on my part, but they both knew that I was reacting to Bob's complaint about having to devote so much time to my grievances against Mr. Gordon.

However, they both enjoyed the show, about Brendan Behan, immensely, and extended their wive's appreciation and their own, and that was that. Tension between the three of us slackened somewhat, at least on the surface.

Harvey Frommer, an English teacher, who had volunteered to be a member of the teacher's watchdog committee, and towards whom I felt quite friendly, as he was a charming and witty guy, came over to my table in the lunchroom, and said, "Say, Fran, I've got some good news for you," in a warm, confidential manner.

"Really, Harvey. That's nice. Let's hear," I answered him, skeptically, yet cheerfully, since I liked this man a lot, and respected him.

He took a long drag on the ever-present pipe he smoked, and said, leaning on his elbows and speaking softly, "Listen, we met with your department and they said they'd stop if you'd stop. We asked them why they were ganging up on you and Ashepa said you always turn your back on the rest of the department at its meetings but they'd be......"

"What! Stop what, Harvey?" I interrupted him, "They're writing letters about me, they're soliciting letters from my kids and I should stop! Stop what? Protesting against such outrageous behavior? Ashepa is a liar as you already know, so I don't have to tell you that what she said about my turning my back on the teachers and her at department meetings is a goddam lie. I simply sit at my desk, and take notes and listen there, instead of sitting at the big table she sets up in the office. C'mon down to my office, Harvey, and I'll show you that she's lying." I felt so angry then that the tears just spilled out.

Harvey was moved by my angry retort to his goodwill offer, but could say nothing more to me than. "I'm sorry, Fran. I thought you'd be pleased. But when I listen to you, I guess you're right, after all, and I'll ask Abe to speak to you later today. He'll tell you the rest of it." He puffed away on his pipe and waited for me to reply.

"Thanks anyway, Harvey. You tried, at least, but Ashepa is a gung ho bitch, and will do anything, apparently, and Gordon is using her to harass me, and I wish you people on the faculty would wake up, because you may be next, Harvey. This is dirty business."

"Yeah, Fran. I can see that, but take it easy, huh? I'm on your side. See you later," he said, and dashed off to his next class.

So the faculty committee had met, I mused, on my way to my hygiene class. I wonder what else came out of the meeting. I found out the rest of the details, at the clock, at the end of the day.

"Over here, Fran, I've been waiting for you," Abe Gerewitz said, quietly, with an apprehensive look on his face. "Want to talk here or in a nearby empty classroom?"

"Let's punch out and sit in an empty room. I'd like you to tell me the whole story, please! O.K?"

"Fine, Fran," he agreed. "Let me grab the stuff in my letterbox and here's yours, while I'm at it." He reached in and scooped up the myriad papers and handed me the pile. I didn't even bother to scan all the stuff, but just threw it into my shoulder bag and followed Abe to a room around the corner.

"Fran," Abe began, haltingly, "Harvey told me he saw you today and told you what your department said. Right?"

"Yes, Abe, he did," I answered. "Let's hear the rest of it," please, Abe. I'm very curious."

"Right, Fran. Well, we saw a letter that Gordon had sent to your department ordering that everything that concerns Miss Newman must be put into writing," he began, looking directly at me, "and so they felt that they were only following the principal's orders."

"Oh, so that's the gimmick, eh?" I countered. "What else, Abe?"

"Well, Fran," Abe began again, "Ashepa's attitude is that you are a terrible person and that she is following the principal's orders and other members of your department seem to agree with her and are following her orders. Believe me, Fran, I can understand how disgusted you must feel with the whole mess. The committee seemed surprised, too, at the nastiness in your department."

"Abe, how do you feel about it all?", I asked him.

"Fran, my candid opinion is that it is a lousy situation. I am on your side and I can see what you're up against. The pettiness and the nastiness of those women in your department is incredible. Tell me, Fran, is it true that you always sit with your back to them all when there's a department meeting? I couldn't believe it, but Ashepa made a big point of it in front of the committee and I was just wondering."

I heard what he said, and again, disappointment flooded through me because Abe didn't immediately come to my defense based on knowing me for many years, but he had to ask me first in order to really believe me.

"No, Abe," I replied to him, in a flat voice, "I never have done that. Come on down to my office for a second and I'll show you where I sit and you can judge for yourself. How about right now?"

"Fine, let's go. I've got time today," he agreed, and we went to the Health Education office. There were two teachers in the office whom I completely ignored, as I sat down at my desk.

"See, Abe," I pointed out to him, "I sit here at my desk and pull out the flap here and lean on it. They sit in the center of the room, to my right, over here."

Abe nodded, smiling weakly, and said, Sure, Fran. This proves Ashepa is a liar, although I have not doubted that at all. C'mon, let's go, Fran."

We walked out of the building together, to our cars, and another unpleasant day was over, though a harbinger of many more to come.

Before I turned my ignition switch, I thumbed through the pile of papers Abe had handed me from my letterbox. My eye fell on the familiar envelope, from the principal's office, bearing my name in type.

"What! Another one! I can't believe it!" were the phrases running through my head as I pulled the letter from the open envelope, and began reading another one of Mr. Gordon's phony letters. It stated that two students had complained to him that I was harassing them, because they had refused to keep a luncheon date with me, and that both girls felt I was out to hurt them.

They were not named, as Mr. Gordon's favorite device is insinuation and threat, combined to masquerade as fact. In this instance, I knew that the two girls had to be Lorraine Friedman and Toni Ferrara, and since I had not even spoken to Toni at all, either before or after asking Lorraine to join the group of students lunching with me, I could hardly believe my eyes.

Needless to say, I drove home slowly, and tearfully, since the frustration Mr. Gordon was subjecting me to, was almost unbearable. However, I know I had done nothing, and that Mr. Gordon was a liar and a totally unscrupulous man, and this fact helped me to remain strong and determined not to let him get away with this deliberately malicious behavior.

Bob Arnesen and I went in to see Mr. Gordon and, as usual, it was pointless. He waved Lorraine's scurrilous letter in front of me, and acted as though every word was undeniably true. The girl had lied, saying that ever since she and Toni had refused to come to lunch with me, I made her feel afraid to come to class, and she was afraid she might do something awful to herself. In this letter, she begged Mr. Gordon and Mrs. Ashepa to send Miss Newman to "hell" or "up the river" or anywhere and please don't let "this woman" prevent me from graduating."

I was so angry as I read it, I felt like screaming. It was so apparent that this letter had been dictated by Mrs. Ashepa to give the impression that I was a tyrannical, frightening teacher, at the sight of whom this 160 pound athlete trembled.

In addition, Lorraine complained that I was harassing her by continually asking her how the volleyball club was doing in P.S.A.L. competition, and that I was making trouble for the volleyball coach, Mrs. Arum.

This particular assertion by Lorraine Friedman is the factor that leads me to conclude, undeniably, that Mrs. Ashepa dictated this letter to Lorraine, and thereby attempted to cover-up the fact that Mrs. Arum was getting paid to coach and supervise the club for two hours each Wednesday, but was, in fact, not doing so, yet was collecting payment for two hours work anyway.

As I began to look at Toni's letter, which was a similar complaint, but less vitriolic in tone, I felt an inner shudder of revulsion against all this contrived smearing of me, by using students whose apparent insecurity and idealization of their gym coach was being directed towards a terribly unfair and dishonest act of written defamation of me.

"Mr. Gordon," I began, standing up and looking directly at his scowling face, "I will not sit here and be subjected to your continuing harassment of me. You are indeed, a pathetic little man, in my opinion, who gets his jollies from stepping on his subordinates. Well, I am not afraid of you, or anyone else, for that matter, and it no longer matters to me what you say or have students say, in letters about me. They are all outrageous lies. Bob, are you coming?"

Bob Arnesen was sitting there, listening, but in his usual semi-cringe kind of posture, sputtered, "Yes, Fran, I'll be leaving now, too. Goodday, Mr. Gordon. This meeting does seem meaningless."

Mr. Gordon sat there, rooted in his granite expression, and only a slight twitching in his cheek betrayed any feeling he may have had.

As we left, I began crying and said to Bob, "This does it. I'll never go into that Goddamned office again. There's no use or hope of fair play anywhere."

"Now, now, Fran," chided Bob, "Take it easy."

"Please don't say, 'take it easy,' to me anymore, Bob," I retorted sharply. "You are really no help and your just sitting there, at these meetings, does nothing for me."

"C'mon, Fran, don't be angry," he answered me, attempting to placate my obvious disgust, with him, and the principal, and the whole scene. "I agree with you, and so does Abe, and the whole faculty, that it's a terrible situation. But what else can we do?" He looked at his feet, then at me.

"I don't want to talk about it anymore, Bob. I'm weary of all the talk." I lashed back at him. "You know very well that none of the teachers have done anything to help me. They've all shown their true colors-yellow, yellow, and more yellow, and that really includes you and Abe and Mickey, and Tom, especially."

"Fran, we've done all we can, and you are being unfair. You shouldn't be so hard on everyone. Try to understand Tom Dente's position. He's eligible to become the head of all the grade advisers and he doesn't want to jeopardize his position, by appearing to be too friendly with you. But you know he's on your side, and that he's a good UFT member, but he's in a......"

I interrupted Bob's harangue and threatened to throw up all over the place, unless he stopped alibi-ing and apologizing for the UFT committee members, whose weakness and "me first and you later" attitudes were becoming more and more apparent.

"You make me sick, Bob. Tom hardly speaks to me anymore, literally ignores me, and I'm supposed to realize that he's really on my side and wants to help, but he doesn't want Mr. Gordon to know that he's sympathetic, so I should try to understand his difficult position. Baloney! Your lack of feeling is unbelievable, Bob. I can't stand it another minute! I'm going home," I spluttered angrily, at him.

"Fran, I do understand, but my hands are tied." he argued. "I'm only a teacher, after all, right? What else do you expect, for God's sake," he whined, trying terribly hard to look big, but his smallness only intensified with this tactic.

"First of all, Bob, you could cancel any plans for the usual end term faculty party and let Mr. Gordon know why there would be no faculty get-together this particular term," I suggested, watching the statement sink into his expression. "And you could call Tom Pappas and ask for a meeting with Mr. Gordon and the chapter and make a firm stand against what he's been doing to me. You could invite the press in and some parents, right? Tell it all, expose this petty, mean monster for what he is. He'd probably have a stroke on the spot, and stop all this harassment, at once. Right, Bob? Hmmm?"

Bob looked somber, rubbed his forehead, swallowed a few times, rubbed the nape of his neck, scratched his head a few times and then, finally, said, "Yes, I suppose so. I'll talk to Abe and Mickey about the current status of plans for an end-term party. It's not a bad idea not to hold the luncheon this year. I could agree to that, I think,

OKAY, Fran, I'll let you know. Go on home, now, and get some rest."

"Sure, Bob, sure," I answered him, "I'm on my way."

On my way home that evening, I made my decision to stay home from school the following week, beginning Tuesday, June 2 through Friday, June 5, so as to shorten my remaining stay at this school.

I would prepare all my end-term reports and grades well ahead of time, and absent myself from the school to relieve the pressure on me.

This decision made, I felt much better and wended my way home through the Van Wyck Expressway evening traffic snarl.

Chapter Twelve

Two More Forced Exams
Compliments of the Board of Education

TWO MORE FORCED EXAMS – COMPLIMENTS OF
THE BOARD OF EDUCATION

The tempo of the harassment campaign continued its cyclone pace now, as it was during this month that I was ordered to go to the office of Dr. Morris Isenberg, for a psychiatric examination. Eugene Kaufman, the U.F.T. house counsel, said I had to submit to this examination, or face probable charges of insubordination. Charlie Loiacono, my field representative, was accompanying me, as my witness, and I was assured that this was all part of the procedure. When I mentioned to Charlie that I was surprised and puzzled by the letter ordering me to appear at Dr. Isenberg's office, he told me that the two physicians who had examined me in February, had recommended that I see a psychiatrist. He explained to me that this was the procedure generally followed, and it was not necessarily anything to be worried about, so, innocently, and as I subsequently came to realize, stupidly, I concurred and appeared at Dr. Isenberg's office, at ten minutes to nine on a sunny April morning.

The doctor was an elderly man, somewhere in his sixties, grey-haired, pudgy, and emanated an old-world aura which proved accurate when he began to speak. "So, you are Miss Newman, eh! And what is your name, sir?" he asked Charlie, in a thick, German or perhaps Viennese accent, as he wrote on his pad.

As Charlie told him his name, and spelled it for him, I noticed a copy of Mr. Gordon's letter propped up on the desk, and I knew that the doctor had already received a false picture of me, because Mr. Gordon lied and distorted and anyone who read the letter would get a false impression. Naturally! That was my principal's intention. Why am I belaboring this point, dear reader? Well, every time I think of that letter, written in 1970, and here I sit at my typewriter 10 years later, putting this book together, I become angry and heartsick, because I am still waiting for a hearing, at which I can present my side of that letter. It is so unfair that I am wincing with frustration, as this sentence takes shape amidst the dancing keys.

Did Dr. Isenberg conduct the psychiatric interview or did he conduct a question and answer session on the statements made by the principal? With the exception of about ten minutes worth of asking me who the president was and what day it was and the sum of groups of numbers he rattled off, etc., the latter is the answer to this question. Charlie tried to help matters along, by asking the psychiatrist if he was familiar with the climate in the American high schools today, since his earlier education was obviously European. The doctor conceded that he didn't really know from first hand experience but that he had talked with many people and knew many people in the school system and he thought that he was knowledgeable enough to know what was going on in the schools. When he asked me the question, "Why did you fail 75 students?" and assumed that because it was written in a principal's request that this teacher be examined, that I had actually done so, I objected.

"Dr. Isenberg," I said, directly, "The letter is one big lie. It's full of distortions and exaggerations. The principal took a lot of hearsay, plus his opinions based on that, and came up with this letter. It's outrageous, every line in it. He never once observed my classes."

"I see, I see," the doctor mused, jotting notes on his pad. "But suppose you tell me in your own words, O.K. Then I see better."

"All right, doctor," I answered, "That seems fair."

"Yes, I failed 75 girls in an early morning gym class, because they either never showed up for class at all, or were late frequently, or did not get prepared for class at all, or were content to just sit along the wall. In other words, doctor, I was following the principal's own orders to do the very thing he brings into his letter."

Charlie was listening to every word and smiled as I explained the failures. This was very reassuring at the time.

Dr. Isenberg seemed puzzled by the facts I had just related. "Miss Newman, you have just said that you were actually following your principal's orders. Am I correct?"

"Yes, doctor," I replied. "That's exactly what I have said."

"Well, then why do you think he is putting this in his letter, here?" he mused, obviously confused.

"The fact is, doctor," I explained eagerly, "that Mr. Gordon is a weakling, and couldn't cope with parents at Far Rockaway, who scream at every failure. He was unable to stand behind his own policies, his own directives. It is so much easier to agree with parents, and attack the teacher behind her back."

The doctor peered at us through his glasses, and grunted the message that he had heard enough on that subject. He was about to say something, but I interrupted him. "May I add one important fact here, doctor?", I asked, "It's quite important."

"Yes, of course, go ahead," Dr. Isenberg agreed, absentmindedly, as he continued jotting notes on his pad.

"This incident occurred 4 years ago, in 1966. It has no place in a letter written now. You see, Doctor Isenberg, I was given commendation for my clerical expertise by my Chairman, Mr. Rommer, in making out these failures. You don't see any mention of that here, do you? Or the very important fact, also, that I received a satisfactory rating for that year."

Dr. Isenberg peered at me, directly, the glanced at Charlie, sitting next to me, not missing a word.

"I see," he said. O.K. Let's go on, if we may."

"Of course, doctor," I readily assented. The interview ended abruptly a few minutes later, as the doctor's alarm clock went off.

"Thank you for coming, Miss Newman. And you, too, Mr. Loiacono," Dr. Isenberg murmured, perfunctorily, as he stood up and ushered us to the door.

We left, and Charlie was first to speak as we walked toward Queens Boulevard.

"Don't worry, Fran. It went along alright. He seemed to be listening to what you were saying," he said, softly. "You spoke clearly and your manner was open."

"I resent the whole thing. And he didn't strike me as being very modern, at all," I replied. "And that alarm clock he had set got me. Not one minute overtime, eh Charlie?"

Charlie laughed, and directed us into a coffee shop near the subway. "Yeah, he sure cut it close. But it's over, and since I've had experience with their kind of exam, I think it'll turn out o.k. Your resentment, I can understand. I'd feel the same way."

"What happens next?" I queried, sipping on a cup of steaming coffee. "How soon can you find out the results of all these exams?"

"All I can tell you, Fran, is that I can call the medical division next week and ask," he answered me, somewhat mechanically, and I sensed the change in his voice and manner. "You'll probably have to get a Rorschach test, too, and then the final results will be issued in one report, after that."

"I get it," I answered him. "The old inkblots, eh? And from all these quizzes, those Board of Education doctors can decide whether a teacher is being framed by an unscrupulous despot, eh?"

"C'mon, Fran, a stiff upper lip, girl. It's not that bad, yet," Charlie chided me. "Some teachers pass these exams. Unfortunately, the way things are, the principals have the power to order these exams and sure, we know they abuse their privileges, but we haven't been able to do much about it, so far."

"Charlie," I began, feeling weary once again, "thanks for leveling with me, but I just can't understand the fact that this forced exam bit has been going on for such a long time. It's so unfair! It's all so one-sided!"

"I agree, Fran. The whole thing smells," he agreed. "But we can only do what we are doing. Listen, I've gotta get back to the office, now. Go on back to your apartment and relax. forget the whole thing for a while. O.K? See you soon."

Charlie left me then and I walked home, slowly.

The next week came and went, uneventfully, and then I received another letter from the medical division, ordering me to appear for psychological testing.

This fourth examination was scheduled to take place at the office of a psychologist name Prensky on East 86th Street in Manhattan.

When I reached Charlie Loiacono on the phone, he agreed to meet me at the lobby of the doctor's office, about one-half hour before the scheduled time. "I'll be in the lobby," he promised.

We met and chatted a bit, and then went upstairs to meet the psychologist. He was tall, in his late thirties, perhaps, and very professional, very courteous and got right down to the business of the day.

"Miss Newman, you sit there, please," he ordered, "and you, Mr. Loiacono, can sit here," he pointed to a chair nearby, and Charlie sat down and the interview began.

"Now, Miss Newman, I'm sorry you've had enough discussions about this letter," he began, in a semi-patronizing tone of voice, as he pointed to Mr. Gordon's letter, propped up in front of him. "Am I right?"

"Yes, you are. Every doctor has asked me questions about the letter, already," I retorted.

"Well, then, let's proceed to these cards. Have you ever seen them before?", he asked, politely, holding a stack of what seemed to be pictorial flash cards.

"I have never seen them in color, before, Dr. Prensky," I replied. "These are the Rorschach inkblots, aren't they?"

"Yes, Miss Newman, they are," he answered me, authoritatively. They have always been used in both black and white and color. Let's begin now, unless you have any further questions."

"No, I don't have any questions, doctor," I said, quietly. I am ready to take this test."

"I'll flash each card to you, separately," he began, "and I'd like you to tell me what you see in each picture. Be as specific as you can. Here we go."

The psychologist presented each card to me slowly, and wrote down my reactions to them.

After I'd seen them all, he read back to me whatever I'd said about each one, and then asked me if anything additional had occurred to me, about any of the cards.

"No, doctor," I responded, "I think I've said whatever I wanted to, except I might add, that the colors are beautiful indeed. Makes the blots much more interesting than the black and white ones."

He smiled, and nodded, as he shuffled the cards and placed them in a desk drawer. He wrote a few more sentences on the pad he had used to record my remarks, and then swiveled around in his chair, stood up and said, "You've been a most co-operative subject, Miss Newman. Thank you. You're finished now."

Charlie stood up, shook hands with Dr. Prensky, and we left.

In the elevator, he said he felt that the interview had gone along nicely and he felt, too, that I had conducted myself well.

"I can't tell, Charlie," I said, "as I've had no previous Rorschach testing, but he seemed like a decent sort of guy."

"Yes, Fran, I agree," Charlie said, "he was very professional. It ought to turn out o.k. Try to forget it, now."

"Oh, sure, easier said than done, Charlie," I lashed back, piqued by his continuing attempts to calm me when I had every reason to be concerned and upset.

"C'mon, now, let's grab a cup of coffee and talk about something else," he said, warmly, sensitive to my sharp tone. Two more months and we'll all be on vacation, right? Got any plans?"

"Right, Charlie, vacation time is always fun to contemplate," I rambled on, between sips, at the coffee counter we had found. "I hope I can make it to June. It seems so far away, every day is a struggle."

"You'll make it, Fran. Just teach your classes and stay away from that lousy chairwoman of yours," he advised me. "And we'll keep in touch by phone."

"O.K., Charlie, I'll try to make it," I said. "Thanks for trying. I know you're doing your best. It's just that I resent the whole business. It's nasty and unfair."

"That it is. No one says differently. But don't let it get you down. Beat them at their own game is what I'm trying to say, Fran." He smiled, warmly, put his arm around me in a gesture of sincere friendship, and dashed off to the nearest subway.

I lingered awhile at the luncheonette, and ordered a second cup of coffee, allowing my thoughts and feelings to settle down into a more peaceful perspective. Then, I headed home.

Chapter Thirteen

Some More Smear, Slander And Sell-out, Far Rockaway Style

SOME MORE SMEAR, SLANDER AND SELL-OUT-FAR ROCKAWAY STYLE

May is usually one of the loveliest months of the year, with flowers and lawns and bushes in full bloom, bursting with gorgeous colors and sweet fragrances. This particular May, 1970, was an exception; for me, it was very bitter time, laced with lies, and betrayals. Its aftermath of deceit combined with events which took place in June, made this final period of the Spring term memorable in its ugliness.

I shall never forget the ambivalent feeling of loathing and relief, intertwined, that I experienced on that last school day in June, 1970,. I left 16 years of my professional life behind me, as I ran to my car. The urgent desire to leave was all-consuming and I yielded to it, as I drove up Cornaga Avenue for the last time as though I were at Indianapolis.

To tell you why I felt that way, it is necessary to tell you what happened from the beginning of May.

First, Superintendent Wilner's denial decision arrived about the 5th of May, 1970. In his decision, he completely whitewashed Mr. Gordon of any responsibility for loading my file with letters, and never even mentioned the Schulman letter, which brought me to his office, in the first place. It was so biased as to be ridiculous. It cured me of any lingering hope of achieving even minimal satisfaction at any grievance in the future.

Bob and Abe and Micky Cohen read it and groaned and shuddered along with me. They passed word of the decision around so that many people knew that Mr. Gordon's letter of lies of April 23, 1970 was used by the high school superintendent to clear Mr. Gordon of any responsibility for his harassment of me. Every U.F.T. teacher had seen the Schulman letter, the Feldman letter, and the Brief and Pino letters, and yet they did nothing. They didn't burst into the principal's office in order to voice their indignation. They didn't try to hold another meeting of the Chapter – they did nothing!

"Wow, Fran," Bob said, "It's really bad. I'll tell Tom about it. Whew, these administrators really stick together. Maybe I shouldn't ask you now, Fran, but…" I cut in on his conjecturing remark, "What is it you want to ask, Bob? What is there to ask?" I said in a despairing voice.

"Well," he said, hesitatingly, scratching his head, "er, do you want to file a Step 3 Grievance appeal?" He was not too surprised when I flatly refused.

"A Step 3 Grievance? You must be kidding, Bob. I'm still waiting for a Step 3 appeal for the pantyhose letter from last December. That's about 6 months, right?"

"Yeah, that's right," he agreed, in a subdued voice. "The Board sure doesn't observe the contract. If you filed a Step 3 now, it'd be next December or so before they'd hold it. I can see how meaningless it all is."

"Bob, can you also see that the whole grievance part of the contract is a farce, too," I queried, with a sneer in my voice I couldn't resist here. "With the Brief and Pino and Feldman and Sheridan letters sitting there in my file, how many years would it take to have all these letters removed, eh? Till 1984, hm?"

Bob had a pained expression on his face. His cheek twitched a bit. He shifted his weight from one foot to the other. His basic decency combined with his timidity and reluctance to act in a strong way were at war, within him. Unfortunately, the weakness won and he spluttered, "Listen, Fran, we can try. I'm sorry about this, really I am, but there's nothing else I can do. You understand. Take it easy, huh? I'll see you around." He left me standing in the hall, and dashed into the nearest stairwell.

Abe Gerewitz also, did nothing but say he was sorry, and Tom Pappas, our district representative, did nothing, either.

Abe was trying to hold a meeting with his newly-formed watchdog committee; they were arranging a meeting with the whole health education department to discuss Mrs. Ashepa's soliciting of letters against me, and the actions of Mrs. Ellen Cohen and Mrs. Carol Husten in the pantyhose mess, etc. Oh yes, from the brief chats I had, in the lunchroom, with Abe, and Harvey Frommer, one of the teachers on the committee, they were about ready to hold the meeting.

About a half hour later, I went back into the physics lab where the meeting was coming to a noisy end, and the teachers were all standing around in clusters, as I walked in. The changing bell rang and everyone started leaving, but Bob and Abe beckoned me to the front of the room.

"Fran," Abe began, anxiously, "we're sending a letter to Gordon, Superintendent Anker, and to Shanker and Wilner today. We drafted a very strong paragraph of protest. Maybe it'll help."

"Yeah, Fran," Bob Arnesen added, "The faculty really feels bad about all this. We'll get the letter typed up and send the copies out to everyone concerned tomorrow, O.K?"

"I don't know," I replied, mechanically, "I don't know if it's o.k. or not. Last January the chapter wrote him a letter and things got steadily worse."

"C'mon, Fran, cheer up, don't be so gloomy," Abe chided me, "Everyone is behind you. Believe me, I'm certain Gordon will cut out all this harassment now that he knows the whole faculty is aware of what he had been doing."

"We'll see," I said, "but somehow I don't feel satisfied with just a letter."

"Have a class, now, Fran, gotta run," Bob added, as he gathered his things together, and started for the door. "I'll keep you posted."

So that was that! I felt let down, annoyed and queasy, all at the same time. I also wondered why no one besides the two chapter chairmen waited to say a few words to me, of support, of comradeship or anything else.

But I went about my business and waited for the printed resolution from Bob. A few days later it appeared in my letterbox, dated April 22, 1970 and strongly condemned the tactics employed by the principal using hearsay and gossip to vilify a teacher, and warned of polarization among the faculty, and urged Mr. Gordon to desist at once. However, I noticed immediately that it was signed, The United Federation of Teachers Chapter of Far Rockaway. High School, without any actual signatures. Not even the Chapter Chairmen had signed it personally. Here was an example of jellyfish-like clumping together behind a formal title of U.F.T. chapter, without any hand-written signatures firmly planted on the page of protest.

I was not heartened by this and awaited further developments. It was not a long wait.

After lunch, I usually clear my letterbox and read the faculty bulletin board, to check any instructions or announcements the administration sent during the morning.

There it was, tacked up on the U.F.T. bulletin board, to the left of the time clock. Mr. Gordon's letter to the faculty in response to the Chapter's written protest. I couldn't believe what I was reading. It was a letter stating that Mr. Gordon had never placed any letters of complaint in a teachers' file without first hearing the teacher's side, in the past, and had no intention of doing so in the future. Furthermore, he had added, if there were any questions, any teacher was welcome to come to his office, to discuss them.

I gasped! I shuddered! The gall, the absolute incredible lie was there for all the teachers to read. And several of them were reading it, alongside of me. Looks of incredulity were exchanged, but no one said a word to me.

By the end of the day, the whole staff knew about it and could hardly wait to meet someone to tell them to read the bulletin board.

I talked to Abe and Bob, and they agreed that the letter was an outrageous lie, but they were not going to do anything more about it. They felt that handing Mr. Gordon the faculty protest was sufficient, and mailing copies to Superintendent Anker, Al Shanker, and Superintendent Wilner was sufficient.

Imagine – the Schulman, Brief, Pino, Feldman, and Sheridan letters were already in my file, and the principal issues a public statement that he never puts letters in teachers' files without consulting them first!

I knew, now, without a glimmer of doubt, that I was dealing with a monster.

When Tom Pappas and I and Bob Arnesen drove into Brooklyn for my Step Two grievance hearing about Eileen Schulman's letter, before Superintendent Abraham Wilner, I had no hope of getting an impartial one, but was determined to fight back with vigor.

So it was no surprise, really, to find that Superintendent Wilner had no intention of hearing my side of Eileen's complaint, but spent most of his time threatening me with charges of insubordination. Tom tried to tell him that the Union had advised me not to go into Gordon's office, alone, because I therefore, had no protection from Mr. Gordon, and I said I wondered why it was so important for a teacher to go to a principal's office, unescorted.

Wilner acted as though we had said nothing. He continued hammering away at my refusal to have a supervisory conference with the principal, without a U.F.T. escort to hear all, too.

He also said that the union was misleading me, because contractually, the principal has every right to hold supervisory conferences with any staff member, in the privacy of his office.

Tom tried to explain that Mr. Gordon had placed many letters in my file besides Eileen Schulman's, and that Mr. Gordon never consulted Miss Newman at all, about any of these complaints.

Bob Arnesen just sat there, listening, and did not say anything.

At this point, Superintendent Wilner stopped threatening me, and drew out a page from his briefcase and held it up before us. "Miss Newman," he sneered, "Mr. Gordon wrote this letter to the Far Rockaway faculty, telling everyone that he doesn't put letters in teachers' files without consulting the teacher first. Surely you've seen it. What more do you want?"

He was grinning, probably the same kind of grin that the unlucky Frenchmen saw on the executioner's face, before he released the guillotine, upon them. Ugh!

I was angry at Superintendent Wilner's patronizing attitude and said so, even though Tom Pappas, the U.F.T. district leader who came along, tried to keep me quiet. I ignored Tom's kick in the ankle, and told Superintendent Wilner that he was as big a liar as Mr. Gordon.

The atmosphere was strained, but Bob Arnesen, the U.F.T. man, did nothing to rescue things. He sat there, mutely watching the proceedings.

I stood up and said quite clearly, "Superintendent Wilner, I came down here to seek justice and it's obvious that you have no intention of conducting a fair hearing, so I'd like to leave now, as this seems a total farce to me. Tom, Bob, are you coming?"

They looked non-plussed, since it's not the usual thing for the teacher to move to leave first. It is usually the Superintendent's privilege to terminate hearings, but my feeling of nausea was taking over, and I knew that I had to get out of there quickly. Superintendent Wilner called the meeting to an abrupt end, sternly, and informed us that we would receive his decision in a few days, and that was that. As usual, at these hearings, Mr. Gordon remained behind.

Another degrading waste of time and energy, but something useful did come out of this April, 1970 Step Two charade. The awareness seeped through me, finally, that there was no use whatever, in filing grievances, since they were total frauds. Later in a coffee shop with Tom and Bob, we discussed the afternoon's meeting, and both men agreed that it was a disaster. They concurred that it was a set-up.

"Yeah, Fran, it's obvious," Tom agreed, dejectedly. "Wilner never even got to the Schulman complaint. Whatta waste of time!"

"I agree with you, Tom," Bob added, while sipping his coffee. "He never even got to the letter. He treated Fran like a naughty little girl who should listen to her daddy. Typical!"

"Listen, you two," I snapped back, "Let's face it. The principal never has to worry about whatever he does – Superintendent Wilner will always rescue him and protect him. There's absolutely no point to filing grievances, as I see it."

"Don't give up, Fran," Tom chided, trying to make something funny out of something ugly." Someday things will improve. Gotta keep trying. At least today's hearing will be on the record."

"Yes, Fran," Bob, the constant pacifier, added. "Maybe Wilner was only trying to save face for Gordon. Maybe…"

I cut in, sharply, here, with, "Listen, Bob, stop the Pollyanna garbage. You saw a total farce today. It wasn't accidental. It was deliberate. It's obviously policy to demean the teacher in a hearing. Remember Superintendent Kole at the pantyhose, Step Two hearing, fawning all over Gordon. Face up, Bob, we're dealing with scoundrels. The grievance set-up is phony."

Bob lowered his eyes, gulped down the last of his coffee, then stood up and said, "O.k. It's over now. I've gotta get back to Hicksville so let's get moving."

Tom assented and we left the luncheonette and drove back to Queens to pick up our cars and start for home.

Tears of frustration kept welling up in my eyes on the way home, and they smarted and burned, but I simply sat there while Tom and

Bob chatted about other things. However, I did tell Tom about the U.F.T. teacher's committee which Abe Gerewitz was forming, to try to prevent situations like mine from occurring in the future, and Bob added that a number of teachers had already agreed to serve on it, namely, Sol Schindler, Vivian Zeller, Harvey Frommer and Leah Schonfeld.

Tom thought the Committee was an excellent idea, and Bob promised to keep him posted on what progress the group made, once it was complete. We all agreed that a faculty watchdog committee might be a helpful tool to keep Mr. Gordon from abusing us, but I was not optimistic. After all, not one teacher ventured forth from the herd and signed the faculty resolution. After all, not one teacher came to see me after the meeting, to offer solace or help. After all, the teachers knew about the Kangaroo Court on March, 1969 and especially, they all knew about Mildred Ashepa's role in all these ugly events, yet they had done nothing. There was nothing tangible on which to base a feeling of optimism.

I shivered in that car, shivered with despair and futility.

After all, with the Brief, and Pino, and Feldman letters made known to my colleagues, as well, what else did the teachers need to trigger them to get together and stop Mr. Gordon?

I couldn't know at this point, that more was coming but since I had recently received a letter ordering me to appear for a psychiatric exam at a Board of Education's doctor's office, I should have realized the horror ahead!

As Charlie told him his name, and spelled it for him, I noticed a copy of Mr. Gordon's letter propped up on the desk, and I knew that the doctor had already received a false picture of me, because Mr. Gordon lied and distorted and anyone who read the letter would get a false impression. Naturally! That was my principal's intention. Why am I belaboring this point, dear reader? Well, every time I think of that letter, written in 1970, and here I sit at my typewriter 10 years later, putting this book together, I become angry and heartsick, because I am still waiting for a hearing, at which I can present my side of that letter. It is so unfair that I am wincing with frustration, as this sentence takes shape amidst the dancing keys.

Did Dr. Isenberg conduct the psychiatric interview or did he conduct a question and answer session on the statements made by the principal? With the exception of about ten minutes worth of asking me who the president was and what day it was and the sum of groups of numbers he rattled off, etc., the latter is the answer to this question. Charlie tried to help matters along, by asking the psychiatrist if he was familiar with the climate in the American high schools today, since his earlier education was obviously European. The doctor conceded that he didn't really know from first hand experience but that he had talked with many people and knew many people in the school system and he thought that he was knowledgeable enough to know what was going on in the schools. When he asked me the question, "Why did you fail 75 students?" and assumed that because it was written in a principal's request that this teacher be examined, that I had actually done so, I objected.

"Dr. Isenberg," I said, directly, "The letter is one big lie. It's full of distortions and exaggerations. The principal took a lot of hearsay, plus his opinions based on that, and came up with this letter. It's outrageous, every line in it. He never once observed my classes."

"I see, I see," the doctor mused, jotting notes on his pad. "But suppose you tell me in your own words, O.K. Then I see better."

"All right, doctor," I answered, "That seems fair."

"Yes, I failed 75 girls in an early morning gym class, because they either never showed up for class at all, or were late frequently, or did not get prepared for class at all, or were content to just sit along the wall. In other words, doctor, I was following the principal's own orders to do the very thing he brings into his letter."

Charlie was listening to every word and smiled as I explained the failures. This was very reassuring at the time.

Dr. Isenberg seemed puzzled by the facts I had just related. "Miss Newman, you have just said that you were actually following your principal's orders. Am I correct?"

"Yes, doctor," I replied. "That's exactly what I have said."

"Well, then why do you think he is putting this in his letter, here?" he mused, obviously confused.

"The fact is, doctor," I explained eagerly, "that Mr. Gordon is a weakling, and couldn't cope with parents at Far Rockaway, who scream at every failure. He was unable to stand behind his own policies, his own directives. It is so much easier to agree with parents, and attack the teacher behind her back."

The doctor peered at us through his glasses, and grunted the message that he had heard enough on that subject. He was about to say something, but I interrupted him. "May I add one important fact here, doctor?", I asked, "It's quite important."

"Yes, of course, go ahead," Dr. Isenberg agreed, absentmindedly, as he continued jotting notes on his pad.

"This incident occurred 4 years ago, in 1966. It has no place in a letter written now. You see, Doctor Isenberg, I was given a commendation for my clerical expertise by my Chairman, Mr. Rommer, in making out these failures. You don't see any mention of that here, do you? Or the very important fact, also, that I received a satisfactory rating for that year."

Dr. Isenberg peered at me, directly, the glanced at Charlie, sitting next to me, not missing a word.

"I see," he said. O.K. Let's go on, if we may."

"Of course, doctor," I readily assented. The interview ended abruptly a few minutes later, as the doctor's alarm clock went off.

"Thank you for coming, Miss Newman. And you, too, Mr. Loiacono," Dr. Isenberg murmured, perfunctorily, as he stood up and ushered us to the door.

We left, and Charlie was first to speak as we walked toward Queens Boulevard.

"Don't worry, Fran. It went along alright. He seemed to be listening to what you were saying," he said, softly. "You spoke clearly and your manner was open."

"I resent the whole thing. And he didn't strike me as being very modern, at all," I replied. "And that alarm clock he had set got me. Not one minute overtime, eh Charlie?"

Charlie laughed, and directed us into a coffee shop near the subway. "Yeah, he sure cut it close. But it's over, and since I've had experience with their kind of exam, I think it'll turn out o.k. Your resentment, I can understand. I'd feel the same way."

"What happens next?" I queried, sipping on a cup of steaming coffee. "How soon can you find out the results of all these exams?"

"All I can tell you, Fran, is that I can call the medical division next week and ask," he answered me, somewhat mechanically, and I sensed the change in his voice and manner. "You'll probably have to get a Rorschach test, too, and then the final results will be issued in one report, after that."

"I get it," I answered him. "The old inkblots, eh? And from all these quizzes, those Board of Education doctors can decide whether a teacher is being framed by an unscrupulous despot, eh?"

"C'mon, Fran, a stiff upper lip, girl. It's not that bad, yet," Charlie chided me. "Some teachers pass these exams. Unfortunately, the way things are, the principals have the power to order these exams and sure, we know they abuse their privileges, but we haven't been able to do much about it, so far."

"Charlie," I began, feeling weary once again, "thanks for leveling with me, but I just can't understand the fact that this forced exam bit has been going on for such a long time. It's so unfair! It's all so one-sided!"

"I agree, Fran. The whole thing smells," he agreed. "But we can only do what we are doing. Listen, I've gotta get back to the office, now. Go on back to your apartment and relax. Forget the whole thing for a while. O.K? See you soon."

Charlie left me then and I walked home, slowly.

The next week came and went, uneventfully, and then I received another letter from the medical division, ordering me to appear for psychological testing.

This fourth examination was scheduled to take place at the office of a psychologist name Prensky on East 86th Street in Manhattan.

When I reached Charlie Loiacono on the phone, he agreed to meet me at the lobby of the doctor's office, about one-half hour before the scheduled time. "I'll be in the lobby," he promised.

We met and chatted a bit, and then went upstairs to meet the psychologist. He was tall, in his late thirties, perhaps, and very professional, very courteous and got right down to the business of the day.

"Miss Newman, you sit there, please," he ordered, "and you, Mr. Loiacono, can sit here," he pointed to a chair nearby, and Charlie sat down and the interview began.

"Now, Miss Newman, I'm sorry you've had enough discussions about this letter," he began, in a semi-patronizing tone of voice, as he pointed to Mr. Gordon's letter, propped up in front of him. "Am I right?"

"Yes, you are. Every doctor has asked me questions about the letter, already," I retorted.

"Well, then, let's proceed to these cards. Have you ever seen them before?", he asked, politely, holding a stack of what seemed to be pictorial flash cards.

"I have never seen them in color, before, Dr. Prensky," I replied. "These are the Rorschach inkblots, aren't they?"

"Yes, Miss Newman, they are," he answered me, authoritatively. They have always been used in both black and white and color. Let's begin now, unless you have any further questions."

"No, I don't have any questions, doctor," I said, quietly. I am ready to take this test."

"I'll flash each card to you, separately," he began, "and I'd like you to tell me what you see in each picture. Be as specific as you can. Here we go."

The psychologist presented each card to me slowly, and wrote down my reactions to them.

After I'd seen them all, he read back to me whatever I'd said about each one, and then asked me if anything additional had occurred to me, about any of the cards.

"No, doctor," I responded, "I think I've said whatever I wanted to, except I might add, that the colors are beautiful indeed. Makes the blots much more interesting than the black and white ones."

He smiled, and nodded, as he shuffled the cards and placed them in a desk drawer. He wrote a few more sentences on the pad he had used to record my remarks, and then swiveled around in his chair, stood up and said, "You've been a most co-operative subject, Miss Newman. Thank you. You're finished now."

Charlie stood up, shook hands with Dr. Prensky, and we left.

In the elevator, he said he felt that the interview had gone along nicely and he felt, too, that I had conducted myself well.

"I can't tell, Charlie," I said, "as I've had no previous Rorschach testing, but he seemed like a decent sort of guy."

"Yes, Fran, I agree," Charlie said, "he was very professional. It ought to turn out o.k. Try to forget it, now."

"Oh, sure, easier said than done, Charlie," I lashed back, piqued by his continuing attempts to calm me when I had every reason to be concerned and upset.

"C'mon, now, let's grab a cup of coffee and talk about something else," he said, warmly, sensitive to my sharp tone. Two more months and we'll all be on vacation, right? Got any plans?"

"Right, Charlie, vacation time is always fun to contemplate," I rambled on, between sips, at the coffee counter we had found. "I hope I can make it to June. It seems so far away, every day is a struggle."

"You'll make it, Fran. Just teach your classes and stay away from that lousy chairwoman of yours," he advised me. "And we'll keep in touch by phone."

"O.K., Charlie, I'll try to make it," I said. "Thanks for trying. I know you're doing your best. It's just that I resent the whole business. It's nasty and unfair."

"That it is. No one says differently. But don't let it get you down. Beat them at their own game is what I'm trying to say, Fran." He smiled, warmly, put his arm around me in a gesture of sincere friendship, and dashed off to the nearest subway.

I lingered awhile at the luncheonette, and ordered a second cup of coffee, allowing my thoughts and feelings to settle down into a more peaceful perspective. Then, I headed home.

Chapter Fourteen

The Final Agonies at
Far Rockaway High School

THE FINAL AGONIES AT FAR ROCKAWAY HIGH SCHOOL

I asked Maxwell Cohen, a member of the Chapter Executive Board, to walk with me to my car, so we could discuss my plans for the coming week. He agreed, and we punched our time cards and walked to Cornaga Avenue, to my car.

I handed Mickey all my required end-of-term papers, which were due on June 5th and later. This was only Monday, June 1st, so there was plenty of time.

"I'll be happy to take care of this for you, Fran," Mickey said, to me, "and I hope it'll help matters along a bit."

"It may, Mickey, I've got to try, anyway," I told him. "Please give my marks and end-term reports to Ashepa, and notify the clerk that I'm staying out the rest of the week, to protest the harassment I've been getting."

"Yeah, I know. It's been pretty devastating," he agreed. "I wish there was more we could do, Fran. Really, I do."

"Let's not get into that, Mickey," I countered. "You know there's lots you should have done, but didn't. I don't want to dwell on that today. Please show this note to any teachers who ask what's going on, and thanks a lot. See you next week. Tell Bob and Abe, Too, that I'll be at home."

I drove off, leaving Mickey with full explanation of my proposed action, and made mental notes of what I'd say in my telegram to Superintendent Nathan Brown, on the following day.

On Tuesday morning, June 2, I dialed Western Union and the completed message read as follows: "Dear

Superintendent Brown: I am staying home from school this week to protest the outrageous harassment I've been experiencing at the Far Rockaway High School. I have been waiting since last December, 1969 for a Step 3 hearing about this harassment. Meanwhile Mr. Gordon is continuing the same treatment and I refuse to submit to this. Kindly do all you can to expedite my hearing, at the Chancellor's level."

Sincerely,

Francine Newman
Health Education Teacher

On Monday, June 8, I requested an absence without pay form and filled it out, writing a note across it to Dr. Theodore Lang, the Superintendent of Personnel, telling of the abuse I was getting and that this absence was literally forced on me by the principal.

Abe and Bob looked for me during that day, and I asked if there had been any problems relating to my absence.

"None that I know of," answered Bob.

"Same here, Fran," Abe agreed. There's been no reaction whatsoever as far as I know."

"Well, good," I said, relieved. "I'll just have to survive the next few days till Regent's week.

"Take it easy, Fran. Vacation's coming up," Abe said, smiling. "And maybe you'll get your hearing before then."

"I'll settle for a reply from Superintendent Brown," I replied. "And a hearing date. Just to get it over with."

"Yes, that would be nice," Bob agreed. "Let's wait and see. So long, now."

I asked Abe to wait a minute, and he did.

"Abe, I'd like you to put a statement into writing about what you and the faculty discovered when you went to my department," I began, having given the matter a lot of thought during the week. "Please!"

He faltered a moment, before answering.

"I'll do better than that, Fran," he offered readily. "I'll ask each member to write a note, too. You mean, of course, about the fact that Gordon gave that letter we saw, to Ashepa, telling her and your department to put everything in writing, right?"

"Right, Abe," I answered him, directly. "I'll need it at this hearing to show the abuse. After all, does every teacher get written up every 5 minutes? Ugh, it's all so-o-o disgusting."

"I'll try to get back to you, by this Wednesday, Fran. O.K? Need a day or so to catch everyone," he said, in a very friendly, supportive way, so that I actually felt heartened by the prospect of such a letter.

It didn't turn out that way at all. Abe found me, in the teachers' lounge on the second floor, and gave me the news.

"Fran, Sol Schindler says he doesn't remember seeing Gordon's letter at all," Abe began, his expression one of strain, mixed with distaste.

"Oh, my God," I answered, in total disgust. "The lying coward! Remember how he had not wanted to go on strike way back in the beginning, and suggested that we all wear black arm bands instead. He even writes letters to the N.Y. POST and signs S. Schindler instead of Sol, in case somebody should recognize him! Actually, I'm not surprised at him! What about the others? Harvey Frommer? Vivian Zeller? Leah Schonfeld? And you, Abe?"

He looked right at me, and I could see he was experiencing great difficulty in composing an answer to my questions, but then, in a kind of Joyce-ean stream, stammered out, "No, Fran, I can't write the letter by myself. I just can't do it. I thought if the others joined me, we could all write a statement that Gordon wrote the letter to your Chairman, but with Schindler backing down, and the others equally reluctant, I'll have to say no to you. Please try to understand." He came towards me, and attempted to put a friendly hand on my shoulder, but I stepped back, and winced.

"Try to understand what, Abe? That you're worried about yourself? Sure, I know why. It's very clear to me," I lashed back at him. "You've sold me out. And I bet there'll be a faculty party anyhow, and you'll go to that, too, won't you, Abe?"

"Fran, please. Calm down," he argued. "Try not to be angry. You expect too much, Fran. I'm doing all I can, Fran. And you're wrong about the faculty end-term party. I don't think there should be

135

one this year. It's wrong! I'll probably vote against it." He looked worn, and tense, but it was his problem, not mine.

He was enveloped in his own cowardice. I went to the teacher's room to wash my face in some cool water, and restore my calm.

Then I emptied my letterbox and found the Regents' assignment sheet, which would allow me to work in other departments for a week, as a proctor or assistant to the marking committee.

I hurriedly scanned the sheet for my assignments and noted them, with relief.

I had been assigned to the math and science department marking committees, and to proctor American history and English exams. It would be an interesting week, I thought, but my pleasure was short-lived.

There it was in writing, on a separate memo.

Miss Newman and Mr. Kerchman were to be released from all their Regents week assignments, to work exclusively on the entering sophomores medical files. They need the time, the notice said.

Another fraud was about to be perpetrated. It was a complete lie, because we did not need the extra time at all.

I did my entering freshman medical screening, during my preparation periods, a few at a time, beginning early in June, so that by Regents week, an hour a day or so was sufficient to complete the 500-600 records.

Mr. Kerchman, however, did not do his medical records at all, but rather sneaked off to play golf during Regents week, and assigned students to handle this chore, and so this extra time was to cover Mr. Kerchman's illegal absences from the building for hours at a time.

I saw this with my own eyes. The boys who were reading other students' medical histories (I object to this) would come in to the girls' emergency room, across the hall, to ask me questions on how to make out the boys' medical folders, and, of course, I helped them. Mr. Kerchman seldom appeared at this time.

I saw red, and went directly to Leon Eckstein's office to protest about my assignment. He had been a good friend for quite a few years, and was a warm, bright man with an ever-present sense of humor, but I had not seen much of him lately, as he practiced the deep-freeze technique on me, just like the other teachers.

I told him I could handle all my proctoring and marking assignments as I had nearly completed my medical record screening already, and this directive was really a cover-up to give Jack an escape route. Leon laughed, grimaced, picked up his phone and gestured to me to wait a minute. He said he'd ask Mrs. Ashepa and let me know.

The note in my letterbox, later in the day, made it all very clear.

"Miss Newman is to have no other duties than completion of medical records for the Regents Week period." was the message.

I, therefore, sat in the girls' emergency room, most of the day, and alphabetized the file on entering students. I also noted that several boys were doing Mr. Kerchman's work next door, reading the medical records of incoming students while the "golfing" Mr. Kerchman was on record in the program office, as so pressured for work on this end-term task, that he must be given the entire week to do it.

I drove to various diners and restaurants away from the immediate area, for lunch, which helped my morale a lot as the days went on.

The "Unsatisfactory Rating" letter appeared in my letter box at the end of this week, dated June 19, 1970. I laughed as I read it, in my car. The bitter irony released me somewhat. The charges, listed below, were not surprising to me, since I knew the solicited parent and student letters were the basis for this phony rating. The letter reads as follows:

Miss Francine Newman
Far Rockaway High School
Dear Miss Newman-

You are being given a rating of "Unsatisfactory" for the 1969-1970 school year for the following reasons:
    Neglect of duties
    Conduct unbecoming a teacher
    Improper handling of pupils
    Improper handling of parents
    Inability to work with fellow teachers within the department

Very truly yours,
/S/ David Gordon
Principal

cc: Dr. Lang
    Mr. Anker
    Mr. Wilner

I showed this letter to Bob Arnesen and Abe Gerewitz, and they were not surprised, either, since Gordon had told Abe he would do anything he could to have Miss Newman thrown out of the system. But Bob and Abe said noting different from their usual, weak expressions of remaining calm, not getting upset, and went on their way.

Neither of them mentioned protesting this outrageous, phony rating, nor did I ask them to do so. I felt hopeless with regard to the efforts of these two jellyfish!

Nothing was said, either, about whether or not the faculty party would be held. I wondered what the staff would do, but asked no one and kept my ears open. Mostly arrangements for graduation were being discussed, and the bulletin boards were full of assignments, seating arrangements and the usual last-minute hectic scramble before the ceremony would take place, the following week.

The seniors were marching through their paces, in the main corridors, and I exchanged some friendly chatter with some of my students. However, in the last few days of my service at Far Rockaway, not one teacher came over to speak to me to offer empathy.

Not one teacher expressed outrage against my receiving a "U" rating, or all of the ugliness that was known. I was ignored as though I had some terrible disease.

Backs would turn, eyes would be averted, whenever I approached a letterbox, a bulletin board or any gathering of teachers in the faculty lounge. It really hurt, but I realized that they were cowards, and preferred to let me be destroyed rather than to possibly endanger their own positions.

This experience has made an indelible impression on me. I shall never forget this shutting out, this expulsion of me, this deliberate non-action in my behalf. Even as I write these lines, 10 years later, I can feel the heartache the sense of isolation and hopelessness that the faculty's behavior inflicted upon me.

About June 23rd or 24th, I received the next letter in the long chain of letters from administrators, arranged to destroy a career, a reputation, a person.

This letter was from Superintendent Abraham Wilner, the Queens High School Superintendent, informing me of my involuntary transfer to Long Island City High School, effective August 1, 1970. Again, I felt a nervous laughter within me, a kind of remote humor.

The Board of Education is doing it again, I thought. A phony "U" rating is usually followed by a forced transfer, elsewhere; the teacher is arbitrarily, automatically, guilty of all charges. The hearing to appeal the charges comes later on, after the guilty label has been neatly tied on.

Little did I know that the hearing would not take place till May 1971, almost a year later. That's the way the Board of Education functions. Undemocratic, unconstitutional, and indecent behavior is their way. They act above the law, as though laws were made for others, not these types.

I told Bob and Abe and they pretended to be concerned, but actually they shrugged and sloughed off this latest assault against me, in their usual, uncaring hypocritical manner.

And now, I learned, too, that there was going to be a faculty party after all, and that my former ally and friend, was hostessing the affair, at her home. And, adding insult to injury, Mrs. Ashepa, Mr. Gordon's hatchetwoman, was assisting with the festivities.

Yes, Abe was going, after all. "Sorry, Fran, but try to understand. You do understand, don't you?" he whimpered. "I know how you feel about this end-term party and you're right, but I am going anyway." His faltering words and his limpness of manner, denoted a sense of impropriety, but a certain resoluteness as well. Of course, I knew he was solely interested in his impending transfer to Dewey High School in September, and, of course, the principal had to sign the transfer, so this was the real reason. I despised Abe, at that moment, of realization, and still do.

In fact, the day of the party, no one seemed not to have gone. One English teacher, Harold Gellis, remained at the school with me, and offered his empathy and understanding. "I feel very bad at what has been done to you, Fran, and I've really tried to rally some support for you," he said, in a comforting way, "but it was no use. No one wanted to speak up, and I didn't want to do it, alone."

I tried to understand what Harold was saying and by now, I do. He was a decent, genuine sort of teacher, and I thanked him for at least having the decency to offer his best wishes. "Please keep me informed on what happens to you. My wife and I like you, Fran, and wish you well."

Graduation was over, the end-term party was over, the frantic last day of the term was over, and except for picking up my check, the nightmare of this past year was ending.

However, the clerk could not find my check, and I insisted that she call the other high school to which I had been transferred, to see if it had been sent there, in error.

Of course it had been! But the clerk couldn't think of that. I had to wait all afternoon, only to be informed that my June check had gone to Long Island City High School, even though I was not to report there till September. Unbelievable, how the Board of Education functions!

My last ugly memory was that of seeing Bob and Abe and Bob Magdalin, the math chairman, serving punch to the faculty, which they reached for, just before they shook hands, with a smiling Mr. Gordon.

How contemptible I thought! Mr. Gordon lied, wrote phony letters, solicited phony complaints, violated the U.F.T. contract repeatedly, in order to destroy a fellow teacher, of which my colleagues knew about, and had been angry about, and they all knew what was happening to me, and yet, there they were, the conforming jellyfish, smiling at Mr. Gordon as though he were a benevolent man, to whom they were reluctant to bid goodbye.

It was a nauseating scene, and I ran out of there, all the way down the long corridor, yearning for the fresh air outside.

I got into my car, and pulled away form the curb as though it were a life and death matter. As indeed it was, the death of a professional reputation and career which was behind me, and my search for decency and justice lay ahead of me.

I never wanted to go back there again.

Chapter Fifteen

A Joyful Journey to Japan:
Then Return to Nightmare

A JOYFUL JOURNEY TO JAPAN: THEN RETURN TO NIGHTMARE

I looked forward, eagerly, to the summer study program in Japan, as a brand new experience and as an escape from the nightmare surrounding me.

And the trip turned out to be wonderful! Traveling to the Orient, aboard a beautiful Japan Airline 747, was a delightful introduction to the Oriental culture in which I would soon be immersed. Japanese hostesses in traditional Kimonos served the raw fish, the tempura, the noodles and artistic salads that were soon to become daily delights to my tour mates and me. Japanese music filtered through the cabin and by the time we landed in Tokyo, we all felt comfortable in our new environment.

The summer in Tokyo and later in Osaka, Kyoto, Nikko, Hong Kong, Taipei, Macao and Singapore proved to be a marvelous, exotic kaleidoscope of eastern culture. The people, the towns, the cities, the countryside, the foods, the languages, all telescoped together into an exciting adventure.

My courses in Japanese art and sociology at Sophia University's International Summer School opened new doors of understanding for me; the people I met on this trip were varied; from all parts of the United States as well as from Japan, and interesting, and some have become close, personal friends, as well.

The pace of this summer was a fast one, and left me no time to think about the horrible turn of events, in my professional life.

I came home refreshed, renewed in spirit and energy, and hopeful that my problems would be solved quickly. However, as soon as I picked up my mail at the post office, and began reading through it, my hopes were crushed.

There were two letters from the Board of Education's Personnel office amidst the mountain of post cards, announcements, bills, invitations, et al, that greet all of us after many weeks of absence from home. I tore open the letters from the Board of Education, eagerly, ignoring all others.

One letter, dated July 10.1970, from the office of Deputy Superintendent of Personnel, Theodore Lang, stated that, "A report has been handed down from the medical division, advising that 'you have been found unfit to teach'."

The second letter, dated July 31, 1970, also from Lang's office, was more detailed. It stated, "that you have been found unfit to teach for the school year, September 1970 through June 1971, and are hereby being placed on a year's leave for restoration of health." The letter went on to state, "that you may leave the city if you wish," and in addition, "you have enough sick days in your absence bank to cover your entire year's leave."

The last sentence of this letter really deserves special mention here. It states, "Best wishes for your speedy recovery."

I am completing this book in 1978 so you can appreciate with me, the outrageous injustice here. Recovery from what? This simple question remains unanswered in Chapter 15 completed 3 years later, because of the lies, the fraud, the abuse of medical privilege perpetrated against me and by unethical doctors at the medical division. And the whole administrative hierarchy at 110 Livingston Street, works together to ensure that the fraud is carried out. This is the basis of my whole court case, now pending.

I immediately called my field representative, Gladys Roth, at the United Federation of Teacher headquarters. Luckily, Gladys was at her desk and I poured out the contents of the two letters.

"Come on down to the office, now, Fran," she said, in a comforting fashion. "Bring the letters with you, and we'll file the necessary papers. Take it easy meanwhile."

Fifteen minutes later, I was on my way to Gladys' office.

I assumed that immediate action would be taken on my behalf and that the Union would scream about this outrage.

I also assumed that the contract had clauses in it that prevented such treatment of teachers.

And I assumed that the United Federation of Teachers cared about injustices against teachers and cared about the contract being honored, and that its main concerns were about the children, the schools and the teachers.

I was wrong in all three assumptions as will become clearly evident very soon.

Gladys Roth greeted me warmly, and after a brief exchange about our summer's adventures, she lapsed into grievance procedure language, flipping her copy of the contract rapidly from one page to another, as she explained what action we would initiate today, a la this contract.

"Fran, this is what we'll do today," she began, knowingly. "First, sit down and write a request to Dr. Liebowitz at the Medical Division, asking that the medical reports on you on which this leave is based, be forwarded to your own physician. The contract provides for this, right here, see?" she pointed out the sentence and it was right there in bold type for anyone to see. It read: Medical Report and Review Under Article IV F 21-

"The report of the Medical Division on a teacher who was called for medical examination shall, upon written request of the teacher, be sent to the teacher's physician."

"I see," was all I could say. "And then what happens, Gladys? I don't have a physician, except my father. Does this mean a psychiatrist?"

"You'll have to hire a psychiatrist to evaluate you, right now, Fran," she explained. "Why not call your dad, now, and let him find a psychiatrist as quickly as possible, and perhaps you can begin seeing him tomorrow, ok?"

"Yes, that's a good idea, Gladys," I answered. "Dad can ask around at his hospital. Thanks."

"Meanwhile, Fran, I'll get some forms for you to sign as we'll request an ad hoc medical review about this decision too. Be right back," Gladys added, and then walked over to the filing cabinet nearby.

I called my father and explained why I needed to have him inquire among his colleagues for a psychiatrist with whom I could consult immediately. He agreed and said he'd call back within the hour.

It was only a half hour when the phone rang and Gladys answered. "Oh, yes, Dr. Newman. That's fine. Yes, she's right here. Yes, I'm glad you understand. Fran, it's your father." she said warmly, "he wants to tell you good news."

I took the receiver, eagerly, and listened as my father said he had been able to contact a neurologist at his hospital whose brother was a psychiatrist. Dad had called the psychiatrist and asked if his daughter could have an immediate appointment. The answer was yes, and the date set for the very next day, at 11:00 that evening.

"Thanks so much, dad," I said, gratefully. I appreciate your efforts and I'll see him tomorrow. Bye now."

"Take it easy, Fran, dear." he answered. You have nothing to be concerned about. I'm sure Mrs. Roth and the Union will be able to clear this horrible mess up very quickly. Call me and let me know what's going on."

I hung up and Gladys explained the ad hoc medical review to me.

"Now that you have engaged Dr. Valicenti we'll apply for this review. He and the Board's doctor plus a third doctor, mutually-agreed-upon by these two doctors, will review your case and render a decision. Do you understand this, Fran?" she queried, in her gentle, deliberate manner.

"I think I do, but let me read this right now, so I can be sure, Gladys," I answered.

She handed me the contract booklet and I read the following statements regarding a teacher's right to have an unfair decision reviewed:

"A regular teacher shall have the right to an independent evaluation by an ad hoc committee of physicians if the finding of the medical division to the Chancellor has resulted in: (1) placement of the teacher on a leave of absence without pay for more than three months, or (2) termination of the teacher's services, or (3) a recommendation for disability retirement."

"A request for an independent evaluation of the finding of the medical division shall be submitted in writing by the teacher to the office of Personnel within five school days of receipt of notice from the office of Personnel that he has been placed on leave of absence or that his services have been terminated, or that he has been recommended for disability retirement."

"The ad hoc committee shall consist of one physician selected by the teacher, one physician selected by the Board of Education and a third physician selected by the other two physicians."

"The findings of the ad hoc committee shall be reduced to writing and submitted to the Chancellor as an advisory opinion."

"The fee of the third physician shall be shared equally by the teacher and the Board of Education."

"Failure by the teacher to select a physician within 30 days of the receipt of notice from the medical division to do so, shall be deemed a withdrawal of the teacher's request for an independent evaluation."

I read this all carefully, and handed the booklet back to Gladys.

"It seems clear to me," I told her. "But when will I get this review? How long does it take? I want to get back to work and get this forced leave overturned. It's outrageous!" I was getting upset just talking about it.

"Now, Fran, these procedures take time. We'll send your letter releasing your medical report to Dr. Valicenti today and meanwhile, you'll be seeing him for his evaluation." she said. "and we also file a request for the ad hoc review this week."

"But how long will all this take?" I kept asking her. "I'm still waiting for a Step 3 hearing that I filed for 9 months ago, remember? Why does everything have to take so damned much time?"

"Francine, I understand your impatience, and I sympathize with your feelings. You've been very badly treated, and we'll do the best we can, for you," she spoke softly, trying to placate me. Her concern was genuine, I believe, but I was unaware at this point of how little the United Federation of Teachers does, or can do, or actually wants to do; of how little effort is expended on behalf of any teacher, no matter how grossly unjust the treatment given the teacher.

"Let's get your letter out, now, to Dr. Leibowitz, requesting that your medical report be sent out immediately to your psychiatrist," she went on, "and I'll send out a letter, requesting that you be given the medical review. I'll speak to Vito about it this afternoon, and Eugene too.

"You're a fine woman, Gladys, but you're still not telling me how long it's going to take. Please, level with me, now," I pleaded, "And can I be forced to sue up my sick days, and have the Board call this salary payment? That seems completely phony, doesn't it?"

146

"Yes, Francine, this has been done," she said. "You're going to be paid for the whole year while you're on this leave, and meanwhile you can try to have the whole matter straightened out, by what we're doing today."

"But what about my sick days? Why should the Board be able to just take them away and decide when and how I should use them?" I questioned, persistently.

"If you win the ad hoc review, then you can request that your sick days be restored," she replied. "But let's take on step at a time. Here's a pad and pen. Write your letter to the medical division now, and I'll have it typed and you can sign it and get it in today's mail."

"Alright, Gladys, let's get on with it," I agreed. Here is the letter we sent out:

108-48 70th Road
Forest Hills, N.Y.
September 4, 1970

Dr. Theodore H. Lang
Deputy Superintendent of Schools
65 Court Street
Brooklyn, New York 11201
Dear Dr. Lang:

Upon receipt of the notice informing me that you have placed me on a forced medical leave from September 11, 1970 through June 30, 1971, I wish to avail myself of the independent medical evaluation provided in Article IV F 21 of the Agreement.

The physician I have selected is:

Dr. Al Valicenti
37-39 75th Street
Jackson Heights, N.Y.
Phone #672-2666

I request that my medical report be sent to him immediately.

Inasmuch as I have been placed on involuntary medical leave, I expect that my cumulative sick bank would afford me compensation to the extent to which I am entitled. Please advise me to what procedures are necessary in order for me to receive the proper remuneration due me.

Normally, when one is ill, procedures are common place. Since the division of personnel, through its Medical Division, has seen fit to declare me ill, I wish to avail myself of compensation without undue inconvenience.

Sincerely,

Francine Newman

No reply from the Medical Division arrived at either the Union office or my home, or at Dr. Valicenti's office.

I called Gladys Roth and she called the Medical Division, reminding them of my letter, and asking that the medical report be sent out.

Nothing happened. Not a word!

Gladys Roth then sent a telegram to Dr. Leibowitz, the Medical Director, which read as follows:

"Dr. Sidney Leibowitz
Medical Division
Board of Education
131 Livingston Street
Brooklyn, N.Y. 11201
Re: Francine Newman

Miss Newman's doctor has not yet received a copy of your confidential medical report. Please forward this to Dr. Albert Valicenti, 37-39 75th St., Jackson Heights 11372

Gladys Roth
Field Representative"

Nothing happened. The report was not sent out! Our requests were simply ignored.

Gladys Roth then spoke to the Staff Relations Chief, Vito de Leonardis, about the Board ignoring my letter requesting the release of my medical report. She was directed to make an appointment with Dr. Pool at the Medical Division, to discuss the matter. Mrs. Roth made the arrangement for us both to meet at the medical division. I looked forward to getting the report and hopefully, to the end of the whole mess!

But Gladys Roth was unable to attend the meeting, because of other pressing matters, and Vito decided to accompany me.

We were met by a Mrs. Orloff, at the office of Personnel, and I learned that she was replacing Dr. Theodore Lang, who had retired. Dr. Pool, the assistant medical director, came into the small office, where we three were seated.

The next hour was one of the most humiliating ones I've ever spent!

Mrs. Orloff, Dr. Pool and Vito discussed me as though I were not present in the room.

The statements made were, "This teacher is ill," and "This teacher is unfit." and "This teacher is thus and so," etc. Everything was said in the third person.

"But, Dr. Pool," Vito went on in a low, very polite voice," Miss Newman has written a release to you, and Mrs. Roth has called you, and sent a telegram about your failure to send out her report, and still you have not sent it. What's going on here?"

Dr. Pool, a cold-mannered, haughty woman, who spoke as though she were a queen deigning to speak to a beggar asking her royal highness for a crumb of bread looked at Vito, sharply, and answered, "We will not send out the report because Miss Newman has made an improper request."

"I don't know what's improper about her letter, Dr. Pool," retorted Vito. "Miss Newman simply asked that her medical report be forwarded to her own physician, and this is what the contract calls for."

"Oh no," Dr. Pool lashed back, in a most condescending tone, "She asked about two things in one letter. I have it right here. And as you can see, she failed to sign the release, and we are protecting the confidentiality of her record."

She showed us the letter I had written and indeed my signature was missing. I realized hat I had sent her one of the Xerox copies I'd made, and in my haste to get the letter mailed, neglected to sign it.

"I'm the head of the grievance office, as you know, Dr. Pool," Vito added, as he handed back the letter, "don't you think I might have been given the courtesy of a phone call, about this letter, so I could've called Miss Newman in to sign it and get the matter expedited?"

She looked at him, with a piercing glance, such as the hangman might give to his victim, just before tightening the noose, and merely ignored his question.

Vito then went on, in a humble, low voice, as though he were facing royalty, and was a supplicant. I was nauseated by his self-effacing approach. Here is the head man, of the grievance office at the Union, playing this weak role! The doctor is violating the contract, and is being callous and he who is supposed to be looking out for the wronged teacher, behaves like he is afraid of this corrupt woman! If I hadn't seen him crawling before Dr. Pool, with my own eyes, I might not have believed it, but sitting there, watching this sickening exchange, there was no escaping the reality.

This was the day when I began to see that the Union had no power to help a teacher, and simply goes through prescribed paper rituals which are futile, empty, and damaging to a teacher.

Vito continued to address Dr. Pool. "I repeat, Dr. Pool, what's improper? "Miss Newman is asking for her medical reports to be sent, as well as regarding the same letter as her release." Dr. Pool said. "Without a signature, we must protect the teacher's privacy, you see."

I couldn't believe my ears, listening to the pettiness, the lying. However, I was able to maintain my composure as I listened.

"Well, Dr. Pool, what does constitute a proper letter, in your estimation?", he asked her, still in that low, groveling manner, which I found utterly offensive.

"This teacher must sign the request and clearly specify that the letter is a release. After all, this is confidential information." Dr.

Pool spoke in a deliberate, mechanical way, filled with condescension. "We must protect the teacher's right to privacy."

"Yes, yes, we're well aware of this procedure. I'll have Miss Newman send this out immediately, and we'll expect it to reach her doctor's office by early next week," Vito retorted.

I could sit there no longer. My disgust with the proceedings took over hastily. My presence had been totally ignored. It was a dehumanizing experience and I stood up and said so.

"Dr. Pool, I found this whole meeting disgraceful and degrading. Couldn't you once acknowledge my presence here? Did you have to ignore my existence? You are a very rude woman and I plan to fight back. You simply cannot bully me this way. You are also very unprofessional and I'd like to see your license revoked. You have referred to me all the while as "this teacher" as though I were a thing, an object. No doctor ever tells the patient "You are sick, you are ill," right to his face, the way you've been doing here. My father is a physician, and he has been speaking to many of his colleagues about you, and it's going to stop. I simply will not allow you to treat me or any other teacher this way."

She looked surprised, and glared at me, but said nothing, until Vito, apparently triggered into acting like a man, by my standing up to this miserable excuse for a doctor added. "Yes, I agree with Miss Newman. She has been treated very shabbily here today. We at the Union are thinking of making this case precedent."

This statement elicited the following declaration from Dr. Pool. "Now, now, Mr. De Leonardis, there's no need to act hastily in this manner. If Miss Newman feels well enough now to return to her teaching duties, we'll be very willing to re-examine her right now and place her back in school if she's fit."

I stood up again and blurted out, angrily, at the supercilious, acid-charged tones of Dr. Pool. "I never was unfit at all; this whole thing is a fraud. I want the actual results of all my medicals released right now. Who do you think you are to keep the actual results secret and then ask me today, to re-submit to some more phony exams and then you'll try to keep them secret, too. This is America, not Germany, or Russia. Dr. Pool, you are not going to get away with this."

She looked furious but maintained a stony exterior. The pink tinge of her skin and a pulsating neck vein were my clues to her discomfort. Her look of bemused indifference didn't affect me one way or another, but Vito stood up and said, "I think Miss Newman and I will leave now, and I consider this matter closed. C'mon, Fran."

He started for the door and motioned for me to follow. I got up, and walked briskly to the door. A feeling of nausea persisted, and I was glad to get out of there.

On the subway, Vito was very quiet, though I attempted to tell him of my displeasure and despair at his weak, supplicant-like approach. However, he simply didn't want to hear this, and assured me that he was certain that the report would be sent, and all would work out.

Nothing could be further from the truth.

Chapter Sixteen

The Waiting Game

THE WAITING GAME

During this time, Dr. Valicenti had completed his psychiatric evaluation of me, and found me fit and in no need of any therapy. He had seen me 9 times and felt that he needed no further sessions in order to reach his decision. The doctor promised to attend the Ad hoc medical review I was entitled to, as my psychiatrist, and assured me he would send his report on me to the medical division, if this were necessary.

Dr. Valicenti had also arranged for me to consult with a prominent clinical psychologist, Dr. Emanuel Fisher, in order to get a psychological evaluation as well. Dr. Fisher would give me a very thorough work-up, including the Rorschach test, which was the sole test the Board of Education psychologist, Dr. Prensky, had given me.

This testing would give me ample medical testimony to present at the Ad hoc medical review, to which the collective bargaining agreement entitled me. I was eager to meet Dr. Fisher, and arrived promptly for my appointment with him, a few days later.

He was a very serious man, and his approach was very business-like. "Miss Newman", he began, "I am going to ask you many questions today, and ask you to read, to draw, to imagine and to be as spontaneous as you can. Do you understand?"

"Of course, Dr. Fisher," I answered him, "Let's go."

I drew pictures, selected words, interpreted scenes, answered questions, and solved various arithmetic problems, steadily, for an hour, and then Dr. Fisher asked me to return for one more hour of testing, including the Rorschach.

I came back a few days later, and completed the testing.

The psychologist stood up and while shaking hands with me, he smiled and said, "Francine, you are psychologically sound and I shall make out my report on you and send it to Dr. Valicenti. You're an enthusiastic gal, and healthy, and I wish you well."

I was glad to hear this, and replied, "Thanks, Dr. Fisher. I hope you'll be available to testify for me, therefore, on the basis of your findings, at the Board of Education medical review I'm trying to get."

"Of course, I will," he added. "You are sound and do not need therapy, and I'll be happy to appear in your behalf. Let me know when you get the hearing and I'll arrange to be there, O.K?"

I thanked him again, and left his office and walked over to the U.F.T. offices to tell Gladys Roth about the results.

"That's fine, Fran," she said. "Now as soon as Dr. Lang answers my letter requesting the Ad hoc, we'll proceed. Meanwhile, keep busy, and let me know as soon as you get a letter from him. Now you have two fine doctors who have found you O.K. and they can testify at your Ad hoc for you."

"Yes, indeed, Gladys," I added, excitedly. "And certainly 9 sessions with Dr. Valicenti and 2 full hours of varied psychological tests give a fairer and more comprehensive picture of someone's mental fitness, than the 45 minute interview the Board psychiatrist gave me, right?"

She agreed readily, but said nothing more. Gladys gave me no indication, either by word or gesture, that I was pursuing a fruitless course, and that she knew from experience that no teacher ever got an Ad hoc medical review from the Medical division. Neither she nor Vito de Leonardis or Eugene Kaufman, the U.F.T. house counsel, told me that nobody gets an Ad hoc Review because the Board doesn't want to pay for one, and will maneuver, manipulate and do everything to deny an application for this contractual right. How could I have known then, that the Union didn't give a damn, either, and simply filed forms and went through meaningless motions to give the teacher the feeling of action? It is a cruel deception that the Union practices.

I learned this quickly enough, when Dr. Lang's letter arrived. It was a denial of my request for the medical review and used an exact quote from the contract to justify the decision. However, the ruse used was easily seen by me, or anyone else who wanted to see it.

There are 3 situations which make a teacher eligible to be granted an ad hoc medical review. They are:

a) if the teacher is payless for a period of three months or

b) recommended for disability retirement or

c) recommended for termination of license.

I have been declared unfit to teach in July, 1970 and placed on a forced leave, beginning September 1, 1970, for restoration of health, without pay. So obviously, I was eligible for the ad hoc. But the medical division and the Board forced me to use up the 200 sick days I had accumulated in my absence bank, due to having been well and on the job all these many years. So the distortion of the contractual terms to justify their unwillingness to grant the review was obvious. They were calling my own reservoir of sick days, salary, which it is not, and were thereby penalizing me as well, for having a fine health and attendance record.

I protested to Gladys Roth, and she agreed, in her mild-mannered way, that this was unfair treatment and she assured me that she would consult with Vito about this and let me know what more could be done.

Two days later, Gladys Roth phoned and informed me that the Union had filed a grievance about the denial and a copy of same has been mailed to me.

When it arrived, I noticed that it was signed Albert Shanker. I also noticed that this had no significance now, because I had found out how little the Union does, or wants to do, or tries to do, for the individual teacher. The letter stated that Gladys Roth would represent Shanker at this grievance hearing.

So here I was, awaiting my medical report's arrival at Dr. Valicenti's office, and a hearing to try to get something for me, which was already my right to have, and which was being denied through fraudulent means.

I hoped things would work out, but I no longer expected or assumed that fairness would prevail. It was becoming more obvious each day, that the Board of Education was unscrupulous and devious in its operations, and that the Union apparently made only feeble, half-hearted attempts to see that the contract was implemented. I began to see that I was in a horrible predicament and that I'd better start looking for a lawyer.

Also, during this time, the third step hearing for which I had been waiting since December, 1969, 10 months actually, was being held on October 20th, at the Board.

Gladys Roth accompanied me to this hearing, too, and it turned out to be another ugly farce. Irving Robbins, the Board's hearing officer, wouldn't let Gladys Roth use the Lubitch decision, in my behalf, which would have allowed all the 10 letters of complaint in my file to be heard at this grievance hearing, and would expedite a solution. He was a very petty, bureaucratic type, with the vision and view of a dead fish in his handling of this grievance appeal.

His remarks about my pantyhose being torn in such a delicate place, and his insinuating that I was not telling the truth about the tear, showed that he was a very small man.

I presented two pieces of evidence to him – Helen George's personal letter stating that she had never spoken to Mr. Gordon about this incident at all and Bob Arnesen's letter stating that the pantyhose incident was a very minor, act-of-God, kind of thing, and that Mr. Gordon's exaggeration of this happening was grossly unfair.

I also reminded this pompous hearing officer that all of Mr. Gordon's information was based on hearsay, since neither he nor my Chairman, Mrs. Ashepa, had witnessed the incident, and she, being the vicious, liar that she was, had lied to him, telling him that all my students had come in to complain, when I, having interviewed each girl myself, found that not one student had gone in to even mention the incident.

The whole meeting here was absurd. I knew as I sat there listening to the petty quibbling over phrases in the contract, that I had already lost this Step 3 attempt.

Mr. Robbins struck me as a rigid, petty bureaucrat, trying to act like a big man. He was ridiculous, in his questioning of me, and fawned all over the principal. Realization of the futility of winning any of the grievance procedures flooded over me, and I could hardly wait to flee from the hearing room. Besides the fact that a few days before this Step 3 hearing, Mr. Gordon had phoned the hearing officer to say that he thought it should not take place, as Miss Newman was very sick, bothered me quite a bit. Imagine the gall of this vicious despot, to try to have the hearing postponed when I had already been waiting 10 months for it to be held; and to say that I was ill, when he hadn't seen me since June 30, 1970, four months earlier. The other hearing officer at the Board had received the call immediately phoned Gladys Roth to tell her about this attempt on Mr. Gordon's part to have the hearing postponed. She told me she had assured him this was not so, and that the hearing should go on.

Less than two weeks later, the Step 3 decision arrived and I read it, carefully. It was a denial, of course, but several things in it need special mention, so that any doubt in the reader's mind about the whole fraudulent, pre-determined decision may be dispelled.

First of all, hearing officer Robbins ignored the two letters I submitted to him from Helen Georges and Bob Arnesen, which clearly show that Mr. Gordon lied in his original testimony at Step 2, and was still lying. The only mention of Miss George's invaluable testimony that she had never spoken to Mr. Gordon about me, at all, was that Miss Newman presented a letter from a teacher. Not a word about the meaningful contents of the letter.

Mr. Robbins also concurred with the Step 2 denial rendered way back in December, 1969, by Superintendent Kole, that my moral judgment was faulty, since I had continued to teach while my torn pantyhose were visible to the class. No mention, at all, was made of my placing my hand over the torn seam immediately, and thereby lessening significantly the momentary impact of the incident upon my students.

He, therefore, ruled that this letter remain in my file with one change made in the wording. The word "crotch" would be deleted and the opening sentence would say that Mrs. Ashepa was told by the two assistant gym teachers that my pantyhose "had torn," etc., etc., instead of "had torn at the crotch," and that was that!

I laughed when I read this ridiculous part. Then I became angry again, at the meanness exhibited here against me. The deletion of the one word affirmed Mr. Robbins' smallness. I asked Gladys Roth to file for arbitration and she promised to look into the possibility. She would speak to Vito and Eugene, and let me know.

Here was proof again, of the utter waste of time it was (and is) to file a grievance. The hearing officers involved in the Steps one, two and three procedures were all principals, or ex-principals, members of the enemy camp, who cannot and will not provide impartiality, yet this is the contractual structure. And the union representatives of grievances act as the arrangers of failures. They make phone calls, set up appointment, accompany the teacher-grievant to those set-ups for dehumanization, and that's it!

Gladys Roth called to inform me that an arbitration hearing for my Ad hoc medical review would be held shortly, and that she would accompany me, and Eugene Kaufman would be the U.F.T. lawyer pleading the case. Somehow, I wasn't at all heartened by this.

The review was held at the American Arbitration Association offices before James E. Hill, arbitrator. The Board of Education had sent a Mr. Stein to represent the staff relations office, and a Mr. Krauss to represent the principal. Mr. Perella acted as the board's lawyer.

The arguments back and forth centered around the fact that I was being forced to take an involuntary sick leave, and that I had accumulated sufficient sick days for me to be paid for the entire period. The Medical Division's position was that its decision was equivalent to a holy writ, and that the mere fact that the teacher wanted an Ad hoc review, was enough to deny it. The Board's lawyer was antagonistic and belligerent, and was very nasty to Eugene Kaufman. The latter argued my position well. I thought, and simply insisted that I was eligible for the review, that every teacher placed on a forced leave was eligible for this contractual right and the point was argued back and forth, across the enormous table, at which we were seated.

James Hill, the arbitrator, sat impassively at the right head of the oval table, listening to every word, intently, and took notes of the proceedings.

After about an hour and a half, it was over, and everyone left the hearing room.

Gladys and Eugene assured me that Mr. Hill was a fine arbitrator and would render a fair decision. Eugene felt fairly sure that I would win this decision, and would therefore get a medical review. He never said a word about the fact that no teacher ever gets the Ad hoc medical review. He never said a word about the fact that the Union's actual policy was to go along with whatever the Board did and not really raise a fuss. It merely goes through motions with the Board and the Union understanding throughout the dismal farce that it is a paper war, designed to create a false impression of action and implementation of the contract.

I decry this deception, with every fiber of my being! It is nothing more than prostitution – the doctors sell their title of M.D., and the Union's staff gets paid to keep the status quo and frustration going along, to justify its existence.

The next few weeks brought nothing on which to pin hopes of untangling the network of lies, delays and fraud.

We waited for the medical reports to be sent to Dr. Valicenti, and by December 4, 1970, a statement was actually sent to him, but was merely a summary in the form of a conclusion. Dr. Valicenti, in his own way of reasoning, accepted this conclusory statement by Dr. Sidney Leibowitz as a medical report even though I tried to explain to him that it was false statement, designed to have me declared "unfit" in order for Mr. Gordon to have his way. This psychiatrist didn't wish to become involved and felt he was protecting the confidentiality of one physician's report to another, and would not allow me, or the lawyer I was dealing with, to see it. He would not even let my father, a physician, see it.

His rigidity added to my problem, because he was not willing to become involved in the case at all, except to go into court and testify about his personal examination of me, and his findings. So, I had to accept this as Dr. Valicenti's way of handling the matter, and its concurrent complications. When my lawyer at the time, Mr. Z, found out that the doctor refused to let him see the statement from Dr. Leibowitz, the Board's medical director, he informed me that he would not go on with the case, as his hands were tied, and I had to look for another lawyer. He really had done nothing to help me, anyway, and I was actually eager to find an attorney who would fight and care for his client's cause.

A family friend, also a lawyer, helped me look for one and finally, through the Manhattan Bar Association referral service, I engaged William, who handled my early court battles. I'd like to complete this chapter now, without getting entangled in the web of frustration a court attempt weaves about you.

The medical report was not sent out by Dr. Pool, as promised, although a conclusory statement had actually been mailed to Dr.

Valicenti, and he chose to accept it, despite my urgent appeal. So, this was a second defeat.

Gladys Roth began helping me to prepare my appeal from the Unsatisfactory rating given to me at the end of June, 1970, so that we would be ready for the appeal hearing. She said copies of my statements would be sent out to Deputy superintendent Lang's office, now, so that Superintendent Rosenberg and the hearing committee could ready my statements ahead of time. She felt reasonably sure I'd receive notice soon, about this hearing date. So I waited! She felt reasonably sure that arbitrator Hill would grant the appeal or an Ad hoc medical review. So I waited!

The waiting is what gets to you after a while. It is a form of harassment. I feel, to keep a person waiting many weeks and months for a hearing. It is unjustified, and wreaks havoc on a grievant. The spirit of the collective bargaining is violated by the long intervals allowed to elapse between hearings, and their outcomes.

But I waited, hoping, that the end of the nightmare was coming soon.

Chapter Seventeen

Charge Accounts – Board of Ed. Style

Board of Education City of New York

FAR ROCKAWAY HIGH SCHOOL

DAVID GORDON, Principal

Far Rockaway 7-6000
June 19, 1970

Miss Francine Newman
Far Rockaway High School

Dear Miss Newman:

You are being given a rating of "Unsatisfactory" for the 1969-1970 school year for the following reasons:

Insubordination and contumely with regard to supervisors
Neglect of duty
Conduct unbecoming a teacher
Improper handling of pupils
Improper handling of parents
Inability to work with fellow teachers within the department

Very truly yours,

David Gordon
Principal

DG: JF
CC: Dr. Lang
    Mr. Anker
    Mr. Wilner

FAR ROCKAWAY HIGH SCHOOL
FAR ROCKAWAY, N.Y. 11691

September 16, 1970

"Miss Francine Newman, a teacher of Health Education at Far Rockaway High School, was rated unsatisfactory for the 1969-70 school year for the reasons given below.

The School Medical Director submitted a report dated July 7, 1970 which contains the following recommendation:

1. Not fit at present for teaching duty.
2. Leave of absence for purpose of health improvement till June 30, 1971.

NEGLECT OF DUTY

On June 2nd and 3rd, 1970, Miss Newman absented herself and deliberately failed to inform the school. She announced that this was a protest against the principal's harassment, and that she hoped in this way to bring the matter to the attention of the superintendent of schools.

IMPROPER HANDLING OF PUPILS

There were inordinately many pupil complaints and requests to change out of her class. Initially, these were brought to Miss Newman's attention verbally. Invariably, she challenged her supervisors for names and numbers, and justified her actions. She claimed that the students were behavior problems, discipline cases, etc. After a while it became evident that discussion would be futile; in fact she refused to speak with the principal unless a representative of the UFT was present. Consequently, student complaints were referred to her in writing, both to provide an opportunity for explanation on her part and to establish the documentation that she always demanded.

She improperly involved students in connection with the incident wherein her panty hose split while she was demonstrating exercises from the platform. After a Step 2 grievance hearing, she had a group of pupils to do role-playing in which one student was to pretend she was wearing panty hose which had split. She also interrogated students in the class where the incident occurred – one group of students each day – about the incident. She influenced one student to visit the principal to tell him that the students were amused, rather than hysterical.

Despite repeated requests by the chairman, Miss Newman skimped on the seven minute dressing time students were entitled to have. This added pressure and tension, and not only caused lateness to other classes but was not wise from a safety point of view.

Miss Newman tended to "rag" students with sharp comments and sarcasm. For instance, when a student brought a note from home about her illness, Miss Newman said, "I didn't know that your mother was a medical doctor." She is alleged by one girl to have called her a prostitute. In an earlier case, she told a student, "You are sick", and became irate when the child replied, "Look who is talking."

UNSATISFACTORY RELATIONS WITH FELLOW TEACHERS WITHIN THE DEPARTMENT

Mrs. Ashepa, Acting Chairman, reports that the other members of the department, without exception, asked not to be assigned as assisting teachers when Miss Newman is the Health Education 1, or to have her assigned to assist them. She does not hesitate to correct, ridicule, or scream at a colleague in front of the students when circumstances displease her. At department meetings Miss Newman seated herself apart from the group, and figuratively and literally turned away.

When Miss Newman's mother died the teachers in her department sent contributions to the Cancer Fund in her mother's memory. Miss Newman telephoned the organization and requested that the money be returned. She offered to pay the equivalent amount.

INSUBORDINATION AND/OR CONTUMELY WITH REGARD TO SUPERVISOR

After the panty hose incident occurred, Mrs. Ashepa suggested that Miss Newman wear panties under her panty hose. Miss Newman flared up and called her acting chairman a "lousy bitch."

The acting chairman made several unsuccessful overtures in an effort to win Miss Newman's cooperation. In one instance she asked Miss Newman to sit down over a cup of coffee to clear the air. Miss Newman's reply was that she had nothing to say to Mrs. Ashepa and did not want to discuss anything with her.

Miss Newman has repeatedly asserted that she would not speak to the principal, even on supervisory matters, except when accompanied by a member of the UFT.

CONDUCT UNBECOMING A TEACHER

After calling Mrs. Ashepa a "lousy bitch", Miss Newman showed the male teacher in charge of the Emergency Room that she was wearing panties by lifting her dress. The next day she repeated this performance with Mr. Arnesen UFT chapter chairman.

After a controversy with Miss Newman, a parent submitted a doctor's note asking that her child be excused from health education. Miss Newman visited the doctor's office personally and telephoned him several times. Miss Newman advertised her grievance in large posters placed in the teachers' lounge. She exhibited her torn panties to colleagues in the teachers' lunchroom.

IMPROPER HANDLING OF PARENTS

A parent visited Miss Newman during open school afternoon to discuss an incident involving her daughter. The parent's letter attached is self-explanatory. Apparently, Miss Newman mentioned that she was involved in a "suit", and asked the UFT chapter chairman to be present before continuing her discussion with the parent."

MY ANSWER TO MR. GORDON'S CHARGES IN HIS STATEMENT OF REASONS FOR THE "U" RATING (of particular interest: use of the word "inordinate"

108-48 70 Road
Forest Hills, NY 11375
September 29, 1970

Dr. Theodore H. Lang
Deputy Superintendent of Schools
65 Court Street
Brooklyn, NY 11201

Dear Doctor Lang:

This is in reply to the statement of reasons presented by the Principal of Far Rockaway High School concerning the unsatisfactory rating given to me for the school year ending June, 1970.

It is stated as a prime reason that this rating was given because the Medical Director recommended that I be given a leave for health improvement. The "U" rating is dated June 19, 1970 and was given to me before the close of the school year. The medical report was issued on July 7, 1970 and was mailed some time thereafter.

Neglect of Duty – I stayed home on June 2nd and 3rd and June 5th, 1970 (school was closed on June 4th) in protest of

165

the impossible working conditions imposed upon me in the hope that a hearing would be granted expeditiously. All of my grades were prepared ahead of time and the end term summary had been prepared for the department chairman. These were given to Maxwell Cohen, UFT Executive Board Member at Far Rockaway High School on Monday, June 1, to be read to the faculty (letters and data attached). I asked Maxwell Cohen to notify the school secretary that I was not coming in on June 2nd, 3rd and 5th and he did so. I sent a telegram to the Acting Superintendent of Schools and later, when I returned to school on June 8th, filed an application for excuse of absence without pay, to you (application attached).

Improper Handling of Pupils – The statement in paragraph two concerning the accusation that there were an inordinate number of pupil requests to transfer out of my class is untrue and misleading. As a gym teacher in 5 classes each term, I handle between 300 to 500 girls (frequently class registers in the health education classes are well over 100 students in each class, and therefore in 2 terms, I teach between 600 to 1,000 girls. I am either directly in charge of these students, as Health Education one, or as assisting teacher, Health Education two, in 4 classes each term, and am the teacher of one hygiene class each term, also, the registers of which vary between 28 and 34 girls each).

There are 9 such letters in my file from students or a parent. Paragraph two, line 2: "Initially these were brought to Miss Newman's attention verbally." This statement is incorrect. I received xeroxed letters of student complaint letters, ready for signature, in my letterbox. This was the first that I knew of these complaints. No attempt was made in advance to inform me that complaints were made to afford me an opportunity to deal with them directly or to give me the professional courtesy of an explanation. In the case of Eileen Schulman, this letter was in my letterbox when I clocked out at 3:30 on March 21, 1970. I showed it to the teachers around me who cared to read it. It was a xerox copy, ready for my signature to be placed in my file. This same method of notification was used in the Brief, Pino, Feldman and Sheridan letters.

The Principal made no attempt to determine whether these complaints were valid. In these last cases all the "U's" in citizenship were given at the first third marking period and all were based on the student's behavior, performance, medical record and attendance after careful individual consideration.

The acting chairman of department, Mrs. Mildred Ashepa, asked the students to write all of these letters (witnesses will testify to this fact). Many of the letters in my file are addressed to her. My side of these complaints was never requested.

Attached is a letter, dated March 20, 1970, from Mrs. Ashepa to Mr. Gordon requesting that Eileen Schulman be removed from my hygiene class. This letter of request preceded the letter placed both in my letterbox, and my file. At no time, prior to this action was I consulted.

Two of these students, Estella Pino and Helen Sheridan, have confidential files from junior high school dealing with their history of disruption and many emotional problems. A third, Eileen Shculman is a troubled girl who has been consulting with the school psychologist. Toni Ferrara, a junior, admitted to Abe Gerewitz, UFT Vice Chairman, that she was asked to write a letter against me to support her friend Lorraine Friedman's statement. The Ferrara letter, referred to in Mr. Gordon's letter of May 26, 1970, has been removed from my file which I checked on Monday, September 12, 1970, at Far Rockaway High School.

Furthermore, the Principal refused to look at commendatory letters from my students. When Linda Brou, a student in my class went to speak to Mr. Gordon to tell him that she liked being in my class, he wrote a distorted letter, criticizing me for using students or getting them involved "in these matters" and placed this letter in my file.

I believe I have the right to know the name of anyone who is writing a complaint against me, with what I am being charged, and to face my accuser. It has always been my policy to reply to any questions, complaints or suggestions for improvement or performance that are brought to my attention in a professional manner. I feel that a student or a parent, who wishes to complain about a teacher, has every right to do so.

Paragraph two, lines 5 and 6:

I asked one file of ten girls at one time whether they had complained about me to Mrs. Ashepa. The role playing was done spontaneously in an impromptu safety session. The girls who were asked to act out these roles laughed and I injected humor into a 5 minute sequence. One girl remained behind at the end of the period to learn why I had constructed the scene. She was a fine student, editor of the school newspaper, and a Westinghouse scholarship winner, and was curious as to what I had in mind.

I felt impelled to defend myself against the charges and wanted to know why two assisting teachers, new subs, went to Mrs. Ashepa to report me. I wanted to know why they signed a statement for Mr. Gordon. I also wanted to know why Mr. Kobren, the teacher on duty in the emergency room on Thursday, October 29, 1970 period 8 when Mrs. Ashepa insulted me was asked to sign a statement about me. Mr. Gordon was turning a simple Act of God occurrence into a damning indictment. The facts are simple. While demonstrating a warm-up stretch exercise, I noticed that my right side panty hose crotch seam had torn. I made an appropriate in-passing remark, pulled my jumper skirt forward, finished the skill, and stood up. (The skill demonstration took about two minutes). No one seemed to be either embarrassed or upset. The students in a dozen groups of 12 moving across the gym floor doing modern dance techniques were no more noisy or restless than usual.

On the last day of gym I asked 10 of my best students to sit and chat with me. The marks were already made up. I asked them how they enjoyed the class, whether they learned a lot and whether they enjoyed having me for a teacher. They answered openly to all questions, were friendly, relaxed and chatty. I asked whether they would be willing to go to the Principal and say so. I told them it would be a help in counteracting the unpleasantness that had surrounded me about the panty hose incident. Linda Brou was the only girl who went to see Mr. Gordon. She told me afterward that he was very abrupt and impatient with her, and she said she would bring he mother to school. Mr. Gordon said not to bring up her mother and asked Linda not to get involved in Miss Newman's affairs. Mr. Gordon then placed a letter in my file saying the youngster was embarrassed and that I should avoid using pupils in this manner. I was sorry to have placed this girl in such an awkward position. I must point out the fact that Mr. Gordon used solicited letters from students to build a file to support his dislike for me as a person. A complimentary statement from a pupil resulted in another uncomplimentary letter for my file.

On one occasion I also gave Bob Arnesen, UFT Chapter Chairman, about 25 letters of praise from students in my class. These were evaluation type statements. Although the students were asked not to sign their names, many did so, anyway. Bob brought these letters to Mr.

Gordon who refused to look at them. Apparently, Mr. Gordon was only interested in letters that were critical of me.

Paragraph Three: This statement is false. I was spoken to only once about dismissing my class late that was the day that Mrs. Ashepa observed me. After viewing the modern dance performance of 10 competing groups which I felt to be an excellent demonstration of the girls' choreographic efforts, in a quiet, controlled atmosphere, the acting chairman's only comment was, "You dismissed your class two minutes late." Considering the fact that 140 girls were performing, being rated by two assisting teachers and me, changing positions on the floor in a complicated fashion, the two minutes overtime did seem minor in comparison with the student's accomplishments.

I did not skimp on dismissal time. On occasion, when some students get frisky and start running toward the stairs without permission, I hold them back, calm them down and remind them of the necessity of safety on stairways.

It happens, on occasion, in every gym class, during tournaments, gymnastics squad work and dance lessons, etc., when cumbersome equipment has to be put away, etc., that dismissals run late. It is unfair to infer that only I, with deliberate intent, dismiss my classes late. When I detain a class, its for the sake of safety, to assure an orderly dismissal. If some students fail to heed a whistle, I must remind them of the importance of becoming quiet and orderly when I blow it. It is with seasoned experienced, professional judgment that I have on occasion been forced to dismiss a class a minute or two late so that everyone in that moving stream of students will get to the locker room safely.

Paragraph four: I never called anyone a prostitute. Mr. Gordon has made an allegation without supporting data.

I read hundreds of excuse notes each term from parents asking student to be excused from gym. Some of the reasons are ridiculous, sometimes the notes are in 2 different handwritings. Sometimes the notes are in a childish scrawl and upon questioning, I have found that the girl has written the note herself and signed her mother's name.

I do not rag students. Frequently, I make jokes of such a situation. When I feel that the moment calls for humor, I use it. I have said to more than one student in the past 25 years of teaching, after reading thousands of notes of varying symptoms, pleas, truths and escape techniques (from getting prepared for gym and actually doing work) "I didn't know your mother was a medical doctor." This comment might follow an excuse claming the girl has a dislocated semilunar cartilage with chips of the patella in the left knee area. Since a lay parent is claiming a very complicated injury and requests an excuse for long duration, I question it and ask for a physician's note.

In technical medical terms, to increase my ability to deal with students' physical problems, I have frequently consulted with my father, a medical doctor, on a number of occasions made it possible for me to gain insight into adolescent physical defects and help me assist them in correcting these.

<u>Unsatisfactory Relations with Fellow Teachers within the Department</u> - Paragraph one. I called Mrs. Evelyn Leys, a teacher at Far Rockaway High School and member of the health education department, whom I have known since I first came to Far Rockaway High School as a substitute in 1945 and with whom I have worked for the past 16 years, on Friday evening, September 18, 1970 at her home. I read to her what Mrs. Ashepa claims represents the request of other member of the department

"without" exception. Mrs. Leys said, "I never said any such thing. You know I wouldn't do that, Fran." I told her that I felt it was a lie and called to confirm my feelings.

Line 4: I deny this absolutely. I show professional courtesy to my colleagues and would never correct or ridicule them before students.

Lines 5 and 6: At department meetings in the Spring Term, I sat at my own desk, facing the table in the middle of the room and listened to the meeting. I have said openly to Mr. Gordon, Mrs. Ashepa and the UFT Chapter Chairman that I do not respect Mrs. Ashepa, that I consider he to be a dishonest bully and wish to have only the most necessary minimal professional relationship possible. I saw her begin to fill out and forge a doctor's name on a green absence form for a substitute teacher in June, 1968 because the teacher, Mrs. Carole Husten, had to get her two children off to camp and didn't get to see the doctor herself. The payroll clerk had said that the teacher wouldn't be paid so Mrs. Ashepa said, "Here, give it to me. I'll take care of it." As she began to fill out the form, I said, "Please don't do that in front of me, as I couldn't ever respect or trust you again." The two of them left the health education office and I do not know what transpired thereafter. I told Mr. Gordon in the presence of Bob Arnesen in January 1969 that I objected to Mrs. Ashepa's assignment as acting chairman of the girls health education department beginning February 1969. The above reason was primary in my objection to her being made Acting-chairman, but, also, it is customary to ask people who have seniority, and the necessary competence, of course. There were three other health education teachers who have been members of the Department for 20 years or more, who were not given the courtesy of the offer to assume the acting chairmanship while Bob Rommer, the chairman of both departments went on sabbatical for the spring term. (See letter attached from Mr. Rommer, Paragraph 2). Mrs. Ashepa came to the

Department about 1964 or 1965, and was therefore the 4th person seniority-wise who might have been considered as candidate for the temporary position.

Mr. Gordon was extremely rude and ordered us out of his office.

Page two, Paragraph two: My feelings toward my mother's death are personal and private. For members of my department to have sent a donation in my mother's memory when they had expressed unsupported derogatory statements against me while my mother was dying of a brain tumor represents hypocrisy. My acting chairman, Mrs. Ashepa, had been making my working conditions almost unbearable, some of my colleagues were assisting her in this endeavor. Their donation after my mother's death neither provided me with comfort nor compensation for the pain they had caused. I discussed this matter with my family. We considered it to be in very bad taste, and therefore, did not wish to accept it.

Insubordination and/or contumely with Regard to Supervisors

Page two – Paragraph three: This incident was taken out of context and is distorted. Mrs. Ashepa did not make a suggestion she insulted and humiliated me in a deliberate manner saying, "you are the laughing stock of the school—etc." "You are sick, sick." In response to her nasty words and after extreme provocation. I replied in kind.

Paragraph four: After Mrs. Ashepa's derisive and hostile actions, I stated openly to he and the Chapter Chairman and to Mr. Gordon, that I was not interested in a social relationship with her and was only concerned with teaching my classes to the best of my ability. Daily instructions were given to department members on mimeographed sheets and also were written on a large blackboard placed on front wall of the Health Education office for daily directions, changes, etc. I attended all departmental and staff conferences.

Paragraph five: After the Kangaroo Court scene on March 21, 1969, to protect my rights, my union advisers suggested that I ask the Chapter Chairman to accompany me to the Principal's office whenever I was summoned.

Conduct Unbecoming a Teacher

Page 25, Paragraph six, lines 1,2, and 3: This is a gross exaggeration of the facts. This entire incident occurred on, the one day, during one period – Period 8, October 29, 1970, within one half hour. The first incident was done with humor and modesty. It was in no way a lewd or obscene act. Only my hose were exposed, not my panty area. The other was a display of the panty hose themselves in an attempt to clear the air and against the Chapter Chairman with the facts since he was going to represent me at the grievance conference. (See attached letter).

Conduct unbecoming a Teacher

Page two, Paragraph 7 and 8. These two accusations refer to the same incident, the same student and same parent. There was no controversy. A parent, Mrs. Feldman, was making a scene. I left the seat at my desk in the first row to fetch a colleague, Bob Arnesen, to act as witness. When Bob and I returned to the room about 3 minutes later, Mrs. Feldman began yelling at me again. There, Mrs. Ashepa came from the back of the room and said. "Another disgusting exhibition on the part of Miss Newman." This was said in the presence of the parent, the student, Mr. Arnesen and me. Then Mrs. Ashepa put her arm around Mrs. Feldman and they walked away together.

The following day, March 24, 1970, the student, Marla Feldman, was absent. On March 25, 1970, I received a note from Mrs. Ashepa saying that Marla had been removed from my gym class and was going to give clerical service in Mr. Gordon's office instead. On March 26, 1970, I received a doctor's note dated March 26, 1970 from a local doctor asking that Marla be excused from gym for the rest of the term due to a strained back. The medical excuse was addressed to Mr. Gordon and appeared most unusual in view of my lengthy experience, reading many hundreds of doctor's notes addressed to the school nurse, or health education teacher or health counselor or home room teacher or whom it may concern, etc., but not to the principal. Neither Mr. Gordon nor Mrs. Ashepa ever asked my why I gave Marla a "U" in citizenship.

I telephoned Dr. Levokove only once, the call was made through the courtesy of Dr. Levokove's wife who suggested that if he were too busy to call me, I phone him at Peninsula General Hospital on Friday morning, March 27, 1960, because he would be seeing patients there.

The only poster I made was placed on the table in the teachers lounge, room 203, used only by teachers. This served as notification to my colleagues of the status of my grievances. It was a simple statement exercising my right to free speech. The attached statements were their reactions.

<u>Summary</u>

At no time during the 1969-1970 school year was my competence as an instructor challenged. There is nothing in my file to support an unsatisfactory rating based upon my performance.

All charges have been based on solicited students' statements and distortions of fact by the Acting Chairman, Mrs. Mildred Ashepa. Mr. Gordon never observed me, although I repeatedly invited him to so.

All unsatisfactory grades in citizenship that I gave to students for the first marking period were based upon departmental instructions to do so (memo appended). Lest the review committee see a one-sided picture of my marking system, it must be stated that I also gave 23 excellent citizenship ratings in June and a comparable amount the previous term. The percentage of passing students at the end of the June, 1970 term in both health education and hygiene was 93.5%. I gave out many favorable personality rating forms to deserving students, also. Each teacher is required to make out at least 15 forms each term. In June, 1970, I gave out approximately 70, as a total for the year.

Sincerely
/S/ FRANCINE NEWMAN"

Have you discovered by yourself, the false statements, and the distorted one, in Mr. Gordon's letter dated September 16, 1970? So you won't miss the deliberately devious wording that was used, let me highlight them for you.

Paragraph One – he uses the "unfit to teach" statement issued by the school medical director, on <u>July 10, 1970,</u> as one of the reasons for rating me Unsatisfactory on <u>June 19, 1970,</u> a few weeks earlier. In referring again to the Unsatisfactory rating letter dated June 19, 1970, do you see the deliberate insertion of an event in <u>July</u> being used to justify a rating given in <u>June</u> of the same year?

Paragraph Two – Mr. Gordon simply lies. I was absent on June 2nd, 3rd, and again on June 5th – 3 days, and had prepared all my clerical work ahead of time and given it to Maxwell Cohen, our UFT Chapter executive board member, and asked him to notify the school clerk of my forthcoming absence for the rest of that week.

I did not neglect my duties; indeed, I carefully did all my required work well ahead of time, and prepared a letter to be read to the faculty, as to why I was not coming to school.

Paragraph Three – He uses the word "inordinately" to create the impression of vast hordes of complaints being recorded against me. Not so! There are always a few complaints made, against teachers, and this is only natural. Some are justified. Some are not. But when a gym teacher handles hundreds of students each semester, how can 5 or even 10 or even 20 complaints be considered an "inordinate" number? It's simply a matter of deliberate distortion.

Mr. Gordon misuses the intent of my role-playing assignment. It is perfectly proper to ask someone if she reported you to the principal, and if the teacher can do the questioning in a clever way, what can be wrong about it? We are living in America, and everyone is entitled to face an accuser, and find out the facts.

Mr. Gordon, being the authoritarian bully that he is, arranged for students to write letters against me, and claimed that all my gym students complained about my behavior when my pantyhose seam tore, when it just wasn't true. I asked my students if they had complained about me and they all said that they had not done so.

You have read my answers to these paragraphs, but I am trying to stress the distorted and false impression this principal was trying to create.

Please note in paragraph six, that no names are used. Blanket statements are made, and very damaging ones, but we do not learn who made them.

Which student did I call a prostitute? Who is she? What is her name? Mr. Gordon doesn't give out names, you see, since he makes up his statements.

What is the name of the student I called "sick?" Does she exist? Did I do so? Why? To harm her or help her? Why doesn't Mr. Gordon name her? Can it be hearsay and rumor that he is indulging in, grasping at any straw he can conjure up, in order to weave a deadly tapestry of his around me?

Paragraph Seven – under the heading, "Unsatisfactory Relations with Fellow Teachers within the Department," there are two words which are used, that make the whole paragraph a lie. The words, "without exception," are false. One longtime member of the health education department, Mrs. Evelyn Leys, did not speak to Mrs. Ashepa, at all, about me. She simply never did. How do I know this, you might ask? Well, I phoned her, at home, on the day I received my copy of Mr. Gordon's letter.

"Evelyn," I began, "did you ask Mrs. Ashepa not to assign you to work with me? She claims you did, and I simply couldn't believe you would say such a thing."

Evelyn replied, "You know I wouldn't do such a thing, Fran." Evelyn had been a warm, friendly, colleague with the gentle manners of a world long gone, and I believe she respected me, despite our differences in approach to current developments in the schools.

I thanked Evelyn for telling me this and reported this statement to Gladys Roth. This fact made a liar out of Mrs. Ashepa, with whose talent for falsifying matters you have already become acquainted.

In the next area of charges labeled, "Insubordination and/or Contumely with Regard to Supervisors" I must comment on Mr. Gordon's statement, "After the pantyhose incident occurred, Mrs. Ashepa suggested that Miss Newman wear panties under her pantyhose. Miss Newman flared up and called her acting chairman a "lousy bitch." He very carefully leaves out that Mrs. Ashepa came into the girls' emergency room and attacked me, using abusive language in doing so. She called me "the laughing stock of the school," and said also, "You are sick, sick, sick." I asked her who she thought she was, and how dare she speak to me that way. She then went on to lie further, claiming that all the students in the class had come in to her office, to complain about me. This simply isn't true. I interviewed every girl in the class and asked if anyone had reported me to the chairman for embarrassing and upsetting her, when my pantyhose seam tore. Not one student had complained.

So, it is obviously a matter of distortion and falsifying of events in order to make me look very bad. Mr. Gordon is an expert at distortion, and falsification of actual happenings, and is apparently at his best, in describing and reporting events which took place, in his absence.

He never observed me, in my health teaching classes, or in the gymnasium, and he was not present in the gym when my pantyhose tore. He never gives the name of my accuser, yet makes all kinds of charges.

What kind of school administrator is this? What is his purpose in writing all this fraudulent rumor-tinged material? I am certain that you, the reader, will reach a correct appraisal of this man.

Please look, now, at the last two paragraphs of this statement of reasons why he requested medical and psychiatric testing of me. Begin with, "after a controversy with Miss Newman, a parent submitted, etc., etc..." This is the same parent mentioned in the next paragraph under the heading, "Improper Handling of Parents." But didn't you get the impression that two separate parents are involved here? Of course you did! This was Mr. Gordon's intention. Exaggerate and destroy is the game plan.

The parent is Mrs. Wolf Feldman, mother of Marla Feldman, but she is presented in two different paragraphs, under two different headings, so as to make it seem that there are two complaining parents, indeed, instead of just one, as is the truth here.

Had enough? Oh, I beg you, dear reader. Muster your strength, please! You've only begun to explore the twisted moral fibers of this principal, and his dishonest devious employers.

Let's move on to new horrors!

Chapter Eighteen

Fraud Has Many Faces

FRAUD HAS MANY FACES!

The arbitration result arrived at my home about this time. I dreaded opening it, almost sensing it contents, but did so and found my feelings to be correct, once again.

Arbitrator James E. Hill had denied my appeal for an Ad hoc medical review, citing the actual contractual language of the collective bargaining agreement, as his reason. Since my particular situation did not appear to be included in the actual wording of the contract, he went along with the Board's claim, that I was not entitled to a medical review of my case.

He, therefore, agreed with the medical division, that the sick days accrued in a teacher's absence back can be declared salary, and that the Board can force a teacher to go out on an involuntary leave of absence, and use up the accumulated sick days as salary.

Here is a direct quote from the U.F.T. contract, found on page 52:

"A regular teacher shall have the right to an independent evaluation by an Ad hoc committee of physicians if the finding of the medical division to the Chancellor has resulted in: (1) placement of the teacher on a leave of absence without pay for more than three months, or (2) termination of the teacher's services, or (3) a recommendation for disability retirement."

By claiming sick days as salary, the Medical Division can commit fraud, deny a teacher the right to an impartial review, and us the contract as justification. This makes the victimized teacher look like the one making unreasonable demands, by asking for the rights written into the contract.

I called Gladys Roth as soon as I received the denial, and she confirmed my feelings. When I tried to locate Eugene Kaufman to discuss the matter, he was nowhere to be found, and although I phoned his office several times, he did not return any of my calls.

Gladys conferred with Eugene about what the next step might be, and through her, over my protest that there must be another way to fight back, I agreed to her suggestion that I ask the Board to re-examine me at this time.

Imagine my feeling at being told that the best way was to let the same medical division doctors who examined me last year, and continues to refuse to release the actual medical results of those examinations, put me through their phony routine again! I saw no sense in this, whatsoever, yet Gladys encouraged me to do this, and she said I could continue to seek private advice from my lawyer who was readying my court appeal. Gladys contacted the Board and we waited for a letter which would plunge me into that never-never world of deceit again.

She also suggested that I file again for an Ad hoc medical review because I had used up all my sick days and now could be classified as being on a leave of absence for more than three months, I looked hard at this lovely, capable woman who seemingly was trying hard to be the best field representative that she could possibly be, without ever telling me the real truth about anything. She did not tell me that no teacher had ever gotten an Ad hoc review. She did not tell me that the Union just goes through motions of implementing contractual fragments into real acts of legitimate battle for the teacher's rights. I came to these conclusions from being buffeted about, by the Union's policy of deliberate non-action and non-implementation of contractual terms. I sat in the field representative's office, day after day, week after week, month after month, being flung from one typewriter to another, being advised to fill out this form and that form, and this appeal to this phony, and that phony, while my professional life slipped away in a sea of unworkable, deceptive phases and clauses, designed to deceive and deny, not to grant and correct and implement all the promises inherent in an accepted contract.

My God, what a terrible thing to do to a loyal, active, dues-paying member! I shudder again, and anger and despair well up again, within me, as I sit at my own typewriter, completing this book, in 1988, at the memory of my own naivete and stupidity for trusting the Union with my fate. I can only tell you what actually goes on, dear reader, and you can see for yourself, through my suffering and torment, how corrupt the U.F.T. is, and I urge you to stop paying dues, and expose the grim farce that is being enacted at 260 Park Avenue South, everyday, as well as at the local borough offices. Only an enlightened membership can force the Union to live up to the responsibilities and trust we have placed in it.

"Gladys, you must be kidding," I said to her. How could you suggest I try for another Ad hoc now?"

"Well, Francine," she countered, "since you're off the payroll because you've exhausted your absence bank, it would be interesting to see what the medical division would do, now."

"Interesting to whom?" I lashed back at her. "I waste a whole year of my life waiting for an arbitrator to agree with the Board – and even if I had been given an Ad hoc and the result was favorable to me, the Board wouldn't implement it, right, Gladys? The Ad hoc decision is only advisory, right? How could the Union accept such cruel terms?"

"Francine, don't get upset. I was only advising you to try. If you don't want to, you don't have to," Gladys said, quietly. "I can understand your distress at the arbitrator's decision on this, but it just didn't happen that way. Sorry, dear."

"I'm going to speak to my lawyer today, Gladys," I said to her. I think it's time to think of taking some real action. I'm tired of this endless waiting. It's futile!"

"O.K., Fran, take it easy, dear," Gladys added, softly. "I'll call you or you call me as soon as the Board arranges for your reexamination. Take care!"

The soft, gentle manner of a Gladys Roth, reflects a warm human being sitting behind that Union desk, trying to perform her duties in a kind way, but is unrelated to the harsh, abrasive actuality of the grievance procedure set-up. The cold facts are that the teacher is discouraged and destroyed, piecemeal, a hearing at a time, by the U.F.T., working with the Board, strangling the teacher's cries for fair play in knots of degrading denials, freely entered into by the Union. Instead of screams of protest against the Board's deceptive and unconstitutional actions, the Union representatives accept results coolly and mechanically.

The Board summoned me for re-examination on October 18, 1971. Gladys agreed to meet me in the lobby of 65 Court Street, and sit in on the whole farce.

I felt relaxed, almost indifferent. In my purse, I carried a sealed envelope, containing the report of my own psychiatrist, Dr. Albert Valicenti, which I planned to hand over to the examining physician.

Knowing I had my own lawyer waiting in the wings to start court action for me, gave me confidence.

A doctor came out of a cubicle near us, and picked up one of the folders.

"Francine Newman?", he called out, looking around to see.

"What's this, Miss Newman?" asked Dr. Lazarus.

"This is the report of the private psychiatrist I hired to evaluate me. Perhaps you'd like to read it, doctor." I said softly, hopefully.

"Certainly, I'll read it. Just a minute, please," he said, "I'll be right back."

We speculated that this was probably so he could get permission to read the psychiatric report I'd just handed to him.

We sat there, patiently, awaiting Dr. Lazarus' next move. He returned in about five minutes, sat down briskly, and said, "O.K., now we can go on. I'll read your doctor's report right now."

He read it quickly, and said that Dr. Valicenti had found me fit and in no need of therapy, and he made some notations in the folder.

"Now, let's see what it says here, in your file," he remarked, as he thumbed through the papers in front of him.

"Hmm, here is something from your principal, and here are some letters from some parents and here..." I interrupted his perusal with this question. "Do you see any of my answers to any of the complaints, doctor?"

"Why, no, there's nothing here from you that I can find," he retorted. "But here's a report from Dr. Isenberg. Let me read it now, and we'll see what he said about you."

"Fine, doctor," I responded. "By all means."

As he read the report, I could hardly contain my excitement. Here was this physician reading this "secret" report that the Board doctors refused to release to me. It seemed to me that this physician's face had a question mark on it, as he read on. There were about three pages of handwritten statements that he was poring over. I could see the navy blue ink and the old-fashioned calligraphic scrawl of the writing.

Dr. Lazarus looked up, peered at the both of us, and shook his head, slightly, as he said, "I don't know what is going on here, but there is nothing in this report that warrants your being placed on a leave at all."

"Really, doctor?" I responded. I hid my feeling of relief, although I knew there couldn't be anything there but a lot of contrived gobbledegook, because the whole thing was a rotten fraud started by Mr. Vicious Gordon.

"How about the psychological test report by Dr. Prensky?", I asked.

"Yes, hmm, here it is, Miss Newman," replied Dr. Lazarus.

"I'll read it now. Just wait a minute and I'll see what he found."

Gladys smiled at me, reassuringly, as is her way, but said nothing.

The doctor looked up, his face a bit flushed, with confusion flickering across his features. "I'll repeat what I said before. 'There's nothing damaging to you in this report that warrants your being placed on a leave.' I just don't know what's happening here. But I am going to look into this."

He smiled at me. I returned the nicety and asked him what would he do now, today, right then and there.

"I'm recommending that you return to school immediately, Francine, as I find you to be in fine health. Just looking at you and talking with you has convinced me of this."

He made a few entries in the folder, stood up, and escorted us to the door of his cubicle...

"You'll have to see another doctor, now, as that is the usual procedure and I'm sure everything will work out. Good-bye, Francine, and good luck."

"Thank you, Dr. Lazarus. It was nice meeting you," I said to him, cheerfully, as he had been very open and decent about everything.

Gladys Roth thanked him, too, and we went into the main waiting room again. Within a few moments, we were motioned into another cubicle by a different physician. He was seated at his desk, with my medical folder lying right there on top of it. He wore glasses, had a round, cherubic face with a serious look.

"Please sit down, Miss Newman," he said. "And who are you?",
he asked Gladys.

She explained her presence at this examination, and the doctor
peered at her for a moment, then accepted her explanation and made
his opening remark, which I immediately took exception to and
resented.

"So you've been in therapy, Miss Newman, eh?"

"No, I have not, doctor. Since you've never met me before, don't
you think you ought to look at what your colleague Dr. Lazarus, has
just written, before you begin making assumptions which don't
happen to be valid?"

"I see," he muttered back, peering at me over the top of his
glasses. "Yes, of course. Hmm, let's see what we have here." Then
he made another ridiculous statement and I challenged him on it.

"I see that your mother died recently and you're single. You have
a problem, Miss Newman." he said, as though he had just issued a
bulletin of international significance.

He waited for my answer, which was immediately forthcoming.

"My mother died a horrible, lingering death from cancer. She had
a brain tumor and I have been single all my life. How can you
possibly relate the two? I deeply resent your remark, doctor."

I saw the baiting and the non-medical tactics quite clearly, and
knew what was going on here. But I was not intimidated, nor was I
afraid of this Board of Education hatchet-man. I asked him a question
which he certainly did not expect. I'm sure.

"Doctor, are you married?" I began.

"Why, no, I'm not," he replied, with raised eyebrows.

"What!", I declared, with mock surprise. "An unmarried doctor in
New York? Boy, doctor, you must have a problem!"

He came up with a half-smile on his puffy face. Before he could
say anything more, I added, "And have I got a girl for you, doctor!" I
played the Jewish mother bit.

"All right, Miss Newman," he sputtered, "I get the point. ha!
ha!"

Gladys Roth smiled, too, and the atmosphere changed in that little
cubicle. No, it was not a subtle, intangible change. It was a direct,
about-face kind of thing. A shifting of verbal gears was taking place.

"I see here that Dr. Lazarus has found you fit and recommended that you return to school immediately. Hmm!"

He uttered this statement as though he had just decided not to touch off an atomic bomb explosion over the entire Western hemisphere, after all! The pomposity in this physician's manner was laughable, but not ever a hint of the grin showed itself on my face. I kept a mask of rapt attention on it.

"What have you been doing on this leave, Miss Newman?", he asked.

"Many interesting things, doctor," I answered, directly. The highlight of this year was my summer trip to Japan and Southeast Asia."

"Yes, I know what you mean, Miss Newman. I visited Japan last year, too and enjoyed it very much!" He chatted with me for about three minutes about Japan and its beauty and uniqueness. He spoke to me for a very specific purpose. Then he resumed his role as an abuser of medical privilege. This is my name tag for every doctor who works for the Board of Education Medical Division.

I would not be so sure of this, had I been completing this book in 1971; however, the outrageous actions of the Medical Division in its unconstitutional treatment of me, since February 1970, has convinced me, and hundreds of other people whom I've contacted, that medical fraud is the official game plan on the second floor of 65 Court Street.

Getting back to Dr. Cinque, whose opinion about my medical fitness to return to work in 1971, was being formed in that little cubicle on this day in question, October 18, 1971.

"Miss Newman, I concur with Dr. Lazarus's findings, and I'm also recommending that you be permitted to return to school right now." He scribbled some notes in the file folder, then finishing this, bid us both a "Good Afternoon!"

We left the place as speedily as possible and compared our impressions, over coffee, in a nearby luncheonette.

Gladys felt the afternoon examinations went well, but reminded me that these two doctors were not the final decision-makers. It was procedure that Dr. Pool, and Dr. Liebowitz would have a great deal to say in the matter. Even though they don't see or examine the teacher at all.

Another pertinent point is that neither Dr. Lazarus nor Dr. Cinque actually examined me. Neither attempted even the elementary basics of a routine physical examination. My heart and lungs and eyes and kneecap reflex remained unexplored that day! The doctors talked with me and read some of the previous reports by Dr. Prensky, the psychologist, and Dr. Isenberg, the psychiatrist, but that was all. I spent about twenty minutes with Dr. Lazarus and perhaps fifteen with Dr. Cinque.

I called my lawyer, Mr. Goffen, and told him about the results. He took the position of waiting to see what the Board would do. I was very anxious to start court proceedings to force the Board to release my medical reports, so that I could sue for reinstatement and expose the chicanery that was going on.

Mr. Goffen argued that it would be best to wait and see whether or not I would be reinstated as a result of these new examinations. Meanwhile, he would prepare the "show cause" brief and ready it for filing when we needed it.

I accepted my lawyer's opinion, although I felt I had already done enough waiting to last me a lifetime. Waiting for Vito De Leonardis at the Union office to decide what to do; waiting for Eugene Kaufamn, the Union lawyer; waiting for Charlie Loiacono, my first field representative to file the appropriate form for this, and then waiting for Gladys Roth to file the proper form for that. Not to mention the interminable waiting for this Step Two hearing result and that Step Three hearing on my pantyhose letter for which I was kept waiting for 10 months. The waiting game, I've since learned, is played by the Board and the Union and designed to cool off the legitimate anger of the grievant and thereby put off the necessary confrontation and the inevitable embarrassment of principals and supervisors, who spend most of their time trying to destroy their staff members who are innovative, creative, and possess strong spinal columns.

I was only a little surprised when I received the letter from the Medical Division, ordering me to appear at the office of a panel psychiatrist, named Jack Schnee on November 19, 1971.

I notified Gladys Roth and she agreed to accompany me to this examination. She was not surprised, either, although she had hoped, for my sake, that the opinions of Drs. Lazarus and Cinque could have been sufficient for my immediate reinstatement.

We appeared at Dr. Schnee's office on Queens Boulevard in Forest Hills, and were greeted by a short, stocky man, with a condescending manner. His voice dripped with a contemptuousness that could be felt by an aware person.

"And who are you?" he bellowed at Gladys, right in his waiting room. She explained her presence there. He refused to let her into his inner office, and snarled at her that he didn't like the implication that he had to be watched. She replied that the State education law #2568 provided that a teacher may bring a witness along to this kind of examination.

He spluttered and squirmed and repeated that he resented the implied inference that he was about to do something underhanded and needed watching. Gladys assured him in her calm, soft way that since the law was on the teacher's side, he may as well comply with it and get on with the examination. Finally, after 5 minutes of a most unprofessional tirade on the part of this Dr. Jack Schnee, he allowed Gladys to come into his office.

Naturally, this incident upset me a little, but I felt I wanted to get on with the examination, more than ever, because of his attitude.

Dr. Schnee asked me why I thought the principal was harassing me and why I was having all this trouble. His manner was patronizing and hostile, and rather than trying to elicit genuine information to help him form a medical impression, he tried baiting me with direct statements, as though he personally, had been on the scene, with my principal.

He also had a copy of Mr. Gordon's report in front of him and as is the practice of these Board of Education doctors, accepted the principal's word as the truth. He asked me to tell him everything.

I tried to explain that Mr. Gordon was weak, a coward, who could not cope with the changing climate in the schools, including violence and parent militancy, and found it easier and more personally satisfying to attack a teacher who had high standards and did not walk around in mortal terror of the principal. I explained that, in my opinion, the principal should have <u>his</u> mental stability looked into, since what he had done to me was outrageous and demonstrated his own insecurity.

188

This psychiatrist made notes as I answered his questions and looked at me, directly, a lot.

After a half hour or so, he declared that he needed to see me again, as he didn't have enough time to do a thorough evaluation. I said I would be there whenever he wished, and agreed to return on November 29th, a date he chose.

Gladys Roth agreed with me, that Dr. Schnee had been most unpleasant. I told her that I was going to call my lawyer and discuss the psychiatrist's nastiness. I did just that and my lawyer agreed that the doctor's attitude left a lot to be desired.

"Francine, I'd like to suggest that you bring a psychiatrist of your own with you to the next examination. I'm sure this Board of Education doctor will act more professionally." Mr. Goffen began. "I know of a fine psychiatrist whom my former partner, Mark Levien, knew and trusted. Perhaps you should call him and see what he might say in this matter?"

"I think your idea is fine, Mr. Goffen. Please give me the name of this doctor and I'll call him right now," I replied. I felt a little better at the thought of walking into that arrogant Dr. Schnee's office, accompanied by my own doctor.

"Certainly, Francine," my lawyer replied. "In fact, it is a good idea for you to get an evaluation for this year, from another psychiatrist, so that we can show an on-going record of excellent mental health for our court brief.

Mr. Goffen had given me the doctor's name and number which I immediately called. I hoped Dr. James E. Shea was in his office now and would answer this call. Fortunately, he was, and we chatted for about fifteen minutes. Although he was sympathetic, he said he just could not be a witness for a stranger. He explained to me that he would see me at his office, and we'd have a consultation about my request, and he informed me of his fee. I agreed to come to his office the following day.

Dr. Shea was a tall, sensitive looking man with a gentle manner. He ushered me into his office, and asked me a lot of questions about the background of my problem. He seemed quite interested in what I was saying and feeling and the time just flew. Suddenly, my conference was ending, and he said he needed to know more about me, and suggested another session. I acquiesced eagerly, and even looked forward to my next appointment because this psychiatrist was a warm, caring kind of man. His concern for the patient's well-being showed in his approach. He did not bait me, or make hostile remarks. There was a two-way flow of questions and answers and thoughts. I talked freely, and poured out the whole nightmarish sequence of events which had brought me to his door.

After my fourth session with Dr. Shea, he asked me to bring my whole file so that he could make his decision about accompanying me to Dr. Schnee's office. I asked him to call me and let me know as soon as he made his decision.

He phoned and told me he had completed his evaluation of me and had read the whole file, and would accompany me to my second session with Dr. Jack Schnee. We made arrangements.

Early in the afternoon of November 29th I drove in to town to pick up Gladys Roth and then Dr. Shea. On the trip back to Forest Hills, Dr. Shea speculated as to the outcome of his appearance as my escort at Dr. Schnee's office. Gladys and I both retold how rude and hostile Dr. Schnee had been. I could hardly wait to get in and out of that office again. We were about 10 minutes early for the appointment. The scene that followed could never have been imagined by even a science-fiction writer!

The minute I stepped inside Dr. Schnee's office, he began spewing out his hostility. "Miss Newman, why do you have to have a witness? What are you hiding? Tell me."

Dr. Schnee looked angry the moment he came out!

"Ah, Miss Newman, I see you have brought company again." he began, snidely. "And who are you, sir?"

"I'm Doctor James Shea," answered my doctor, standing up to shake hands, and towering over the short, Napoleonic Schnee. "I'll be Miss Newman's witness today."

"Oh, no, you won't, doctor," he snapped back. "I checked with Dr. Liebowitz and I don't have to have anyone watching me do my job."

"Really, Dr. Schnee, you're being most unfair to Francine." Gladys Roth said, softly but firmly. "The law says that the teacher can be accompanied by a person of her choice. We went through this once before and you really are out of order, doctor."

Dr. Schnee glared at Gladys, glared at me, and totally ignored the dignified presence of Dr. Shea. It was an amazing sight. He looked like a nasty little kid who was about to kick all the furniture because his mother had just told him he couldn't have any candy. Outrageous!

"I am telling you right now, Miss Newman," he sputtered, "that you either come in my office, alone, now, or the interview will not take place at all. Make up your mind."

I looked at Gladys and at Dr. Shea and they both advised me to go in alone, and we would discuss the legalities of the matter on the way back.

Chapter Nineteen

At Brooklyn State Supreme Court
Where Your Fate Is In The
Hands of Those Court Jesters
Called Judges, and the Joker Is You

AT BROOKLYN STATE SUPREME COURT: WHERE YOUR FATE IS IN THE HANDS OF THOSE COURT JESTERS CALLED JUDGES: AND THE JOKER IS YOU.

Mr. Goffen filed the Article 78 "Show Cause" order against the Board in March 1972. Have you ever waited for a Show Cause order hearing in the Brooklyn Supreme Court?

Have you ever watched the callous indifference and boredom displayed by the court clerks as they call the calendar to find out which plaintiffs are actually in court, on that particular morning, and which ones have given up in despair after trying for days, weeks, and months – yes, months, to get a proper hearing, in front of that black-garbed high priest out there?

Have you listened eagerly for your case number to be called out, finally, and then you hear it, and the clerk drones on towards number 115 or so, in a mechanical sputter. Yes, 115 cases on the calendar, all to be heard and dealt with fairly, by a judge who probably bought his judgeship at the local political club, and cares more about money and power than you, the citizen who pays his salary.

Now that the initial calendar call has been completed, the stage has been set for the real farce to begin.

The judge enters the courtroom and everyone is asked to stand as "His Honor" arrives and settles himself on his lofty perch. The cases are called, amidst a flurry of briefs being opened, closed, passed from one side to the other, by attorneys scurrying back and forth from the plaintiff's side to the defendant's side. Eager plaintiffs and belligerent or angry defendants sit nearby, intent upon the proceedings.

The arguments seemed brief and cursory to me. The judge interrupted any attempt at oral argument beyond the mere introduction of the issues which had brought the plaintiff to court in the first place. He seemed to be in a great hurry to finish his caseload.

I got no impression whatsoever of a concerned, caring judge up there, peering down at the myriad assemblage of people sitting there, anxious, upset, frightened, and of course, hoping for understanding and justice.

Since my first time in the courtroom at Brooklyn Supreme was the most shocking, I'm stressing the disappointment, bordering on disgust which I felt then, and subsequently, my visits to the court evoked a kind of numbness within me. A most unpleasant feeling, I must add, since all my life I had thought that you have a problem, you simply hire a lawyer and go off to the nearest court, and appear before a benign judge who loves his work and can't wait to dispense fairness and justice to the nearest plaintiff seeking these elusive results. My God! nothing could be farther from the cold, and in my opinion, phony atmosphere that pervades the courtroom of the Supreme Court structure.

Judge Dominic S. Rinaldi was the first judge before whom we appeared. When my lawyer was called to the bar, the Board of Education lawyer, Mr. Ahrens, immediately asked for a postponement of several weeks as the Board wanted more time, and my lawyer objected – not in firm, stentorian tones as I would have liked, but in a quiet, polite way.

Judge Rinaldi overruled him and granted the delay and we were back in the corridor in about 6 minutes!

Three years of my life, wasted on eleven kangaroo grievance hearings which the Union and the Board held in order to perpetuate the tragic myth of contract implementation, led me to this fiasco. There I was, in the courtroom of one Judge Dominic Rinaldi, who barely paid attention to the proceedings.

And, a few weeks later, a similar farce was enacted before Judge Franklin W. Morton, Jr. After another lengthy calendar call, the Board's lawyer immediately asked for still another postponement! The excuse, this time, was that they still needed more time to prepare their answering brief.

My lawyer rushed to the podium, and attempted to plead for a proper hearing, and objected to the Board's request for delay. He was promptly overruled by this indifferent judge, who granted the delay, and there we were, out in the corridor again, with absolutely nothing accomplished.

Two weeks later, we were back in the courtroom for a third try before another judge. This time the presiding judge was Louis B. Heller. He sat up there looking somewhat alert and seemed interested in what was happening around him. A spark of hope started flickering within me that this might be the day when someone in authority would do his duty, fairly, impartially; a judge would be curious to find out how a teacher with a fine record of satisfactory teaching, could suddenly become "unfit." A fair judge who would want to hear all the facts and see all the evidence, from both sides, before he issued his ruling. Right? Wrong! The reality that occurred in that courtroom makes the previous three sentences seem like the thought of a naïve adolescent.

Judge Heller allowed my attorney to mumble a few words about my rights and then stopped him, in order to allow the Board's attorney, to argue against whatever Mr. Goffen was trying to get across. Then he asked that the attorneys leave all their papers with the clerk, and assured us that he would study the material and render his judgment thereafter.

As we left the courthouse together, my lawyer seemed more optimistic about the possible outcome. He assured me that the judge could get the actual medical reports that the Medical Division was keeping secret, and that he could easily see the fraud that had been committed. However, he added, that he hoped the judge would read the brief and when I questioned him on this, he countered with the revelation that very often, a law clerk actually reads the briefs and makes the decisions. The judge merely affixes his signature, and there you see the seed of abuse of the plaintiff by the judges and the court clerks, as well as by the forces which brought the litigant to the court in the first place.

The judge's law secretary, who does not appear in court, and does not hear the oral arguments at all, may actually make the decision. So what is the point of the whole farce? I was shocked at this new bit of information, yet continued to hope that maybe something good would happen. How wrong I was!

Judge Heller's decision, dated May 17, 1972 arrived at Mr. Goffen's office, and it was unbelievable. I read my copy of it several times, and could not totally absorb the inherent fraud and obvious miscarriage of justice that it was. Specifically, whatever we requested was denied. I had provided three doctor's notes attesting to my fitness, and the Board provided nothing and yet, Judge Heller ruled with and for the Board in refusing to annul my two forced leaves, based on the still unrevealed medical reports the Board said it had. My question to my lawyer was, "how can a judge make an intelligent, fair decision in a case if he is only presented with one-half the evidence?" Mr. Goffen did not have a satisfactory answer. He merely implied that the judge could do more or less whatever he wanted to do, and that we could appeal his decision, to the Appellate Court, and hope for some fairness there. I was appalled and stunned, and have continued to be appalled and stunned at all the denials, delays, and obvious behind-the-scenes activity of the Board in squelching this case. And I have to spend my hard-earned savings to be defrauded of elementary basic decency, besides! Dear reader, join me and let's scream our protests. But to whom and where can we protest? Who will care? Who will listen? Has anybody listened yet, as deception after deception occurs?

I have saved the worst aspect of Judge Heller's decision for the end of this chapter. He remanded me back to the Medical Division for re-examination to determine my fitness and said nothing at all about the fact that the Board had taken only phrases out of my own psychologist's report (Dr. Emanuel Fisher); and used them as "their" evidence to support the medical director's conclusory statement of unfitness, while presenting not a word of the supposed findings of their own physicians. Outrageous?

When we realized what they had done, Mr. Goffen phoned Dr. Fisher and when he heard how the Board had taken his findings and twisted them so that they were complete distortion of his diagnosis, he immediately offered to dictate a statement of protest about this, to the Medical Division.

He did so, and Mr. Goffen affixed this evidence to the Court papers, and nothing happened. It was ignored by Judge Heller. Unbelievable?

And last, but by no means least, is what the Board's Medical Directors did with the statements made by Dr. Lazarus and Dr. Cinque, to me in front of a witness, Mrs. Gladys Roth, as told in an earlier chapter.

Drs. Lazarus and Cinque had not examined me, but had spoken to me, and both had recommended that I be returned to school immediately, as they could find no reason to conclude otherwise, in paragraph 61 of the Board's answering brief. They had said absolutely nothing about my needing a psychiatric evaluation. However, in paragraph 62, the statement is arranged to make it seem that both Drs. Lazarus and Dr. Cinque had recommended this. And Dr. Liebowitz, the medical director, states that it does not matter what the two examining physicians said, anyhow, he makes the final determinations. Then what is the point of going through the examinations in the first place? Do you smell fraud as I do? Do you smell the stench of abuse of power by a corrupt medical director, whose only aim is to serve as an unethical, willing accomplice to the unscrupulous actions of Board of Education principals, superintendents, and the Chancellor?

With Mr. Goffen's permission, I phoned Dr. Lazarus, at his home, to discuss with him the distortions of his findings in the court brief that the Board had prepared. He was very cold, and annoyed at first, that I was calling him at home. I asked him to let me explain why I took the liberty of doing this. I told him that he didn't strike me as a phony, unethical Board-type doctor, and that I couldn't believe that he had said one thing to my face, at the examination, in front of a witness, and a totally different statement to Dr. Liebowitz. He then answered that I would have to subpoena him in court if I wanted him to talk further, and I said that I would do this at the proper time. However, I had hoped to let him know how he was being used by Dr. Liebowitz. I assumed, I told him, that he was unaware of how Dr. Liebowitz and Pool had twisted his findings.

"How could you suddenly decide that I was unfit to teach, after declaring me to be okay to return to work immediately." was what I said. Even Mr. Goffen agreed that something was wrong here.

It was obvious that Dr. Liebowitz had arranged the evidence, to suite his purposes, which obviously had nothing to do with anything medical. Let me repeat here: Dr. Liebowitz's sole role as medical director is to commit fraud via arrangement of phony, damaging statements against teachers, and thereby enable cowardly administrators to wield power over their staffs. He has perfected his role of dictator to such an extent that the mere threat, by a principal, of a forced medical exam at the Board, apparently has squelched most teachers' resistance.

A week or so after I called Dr. Lazarus, the Board's lawyer called Mr. Goffen to complain that I had called him and made threatening remarks to him late in the night.

What a false charge!! Completely distorted to make a genuine concern for a seemingly decent doctor's reputation into something totally opposite; into something unlawful. The gall of the Board knows no bounds.

There I was again - - nowhere!!

My only hope was to appeal to the Appellate Division of the Brooklyn Supreme Court.

I asked my attorney to file an appeal. After about three weeks, the answer came, from Judge Samuel Rabin and two other judges who comprise the 3-man court. "Appeal is denied."

No reason – just a denial. And, I learned later, no reason is required! Mr. Goffen told me I had the right to appeal to the State's highest court – the 7-man Court of Appeals. I asked him to prepare the papers. I was still hoping to get a fair hearing, and a trial, so that my side could be heard.

Two months later, towards the end of September, 1972, I flew to Albany, to meet my attorney at the Appeals Court.

After about a 3 minute conference between Mr. Goffen and the judge who acted as spokesman for the 7-man set up, the entire hearing was over! No one from the Corporation Counsel's office appeared to argue for the Board.

Mr. Goffen escorted me to the outer corridor, and explained the proceedings to me.

"I'm sorry, Francine. Your appeal has been denied here, too."

"You mean, they simply refuse to hear the case, also?" I asked, in a near cry. The disappointment I was feeling rendered me weak, so weak in fact, that I could hardly stand up.

"Yes, they denied your appeal. I'm sorry."

"Why?" I repeated. "How could they? And why isn't the Board here, too?"

"I can only tell you the results, Francine. I can surmise that they don't want to hear the case, and so they've used their right to deny you a hearing. That's the way it is."

Mr. Goffen invited me to join him and his wife for a drink at a nearby hotel, before we flew back to the city. I said practically nothing as we sat there. I felt an unbearable frustration and wanted to sob, but, instead I gulped down my drink and listened to Mrs. Goffen's attempt at consolation.

It did not work. She tried her best to be pleasant, but the disgust I felt far outweighed all other feelings.

I was back to nowhere again! Here it was, 1972, two years after being so brutally treated by my principal and the faculty and the Board, and I had not moved one step forward toward a solution.

Chapter Twenty

"An Assortment of Horrors: Judicial "Dirty Tricks", Unanswered Letters to politicians, Unanswered phone calls, to the press and Unkept Promises from all of the above.

An assortment of horrors: judicial "dirty tricks", unanswered letters to politicians, unreturned phone calls to the press and unkept promises from all of the above

Deafening Silence is very difficult to accept. I was reeling with disgust at the State Appellate Courts' non-action on my appeal. These judges have the absolute power to deny appeals, without having to explain their decisions. They do this even when the plaintiff's case is totally justified.

Sickening! Frustrating!

A few days later, I decided to terminate my relationship with Mr. Goffen; he had no fire, no zest, no real push power, to force the judges to listen to him. He simply recited the necessary statements needed for filing a plea, and leaving it with the judge's law clerk.

Mr. Goffen accepted my decision, and refunded a check I had issued to him, and wished me luck.

I needed some fiery type lawyer to enter the Federal Court arena, and to fight for my constitutional rights.

Fate stepped in when I happened to look at the book display in the Doubleday bookstore on Fifth Ave. and noted the title of the book being featured. Its title Psychiatric Justice the author was Dr. Thomas Szasz, a world famous psychiatrist and professor and author of many books critical of Psychiatry.

I bought the book, and rushed home to read it. I felt a rush of optimism, and hope as I perused the cases that Dr. Szasz was explaining.

The book deals with 4 men caught up in psychiatric enslavement and legal conflicts which violated their constitutional rights to be free......Mind blowing......

As I read the book, I felt chilled to the bone, and, at the same time, warmed by the new knowledge I was acquiring on every page.

A phone call to the Syracuse Upstate Medical center the next day changed my life.

Dr. Szasz was very pleasant and open with me, as I poured out my story.

He suggested that I send him some of my court papers so that he could acquaint himself with the facts in my situation. He said he would call be back, in a few days.

He did call; he advised me to get a good lawyer and to continue to fight the forced psychiatric labeling syndrome that I had been caught in. He explained that forced labeling, and forced commitment and denial of due process to many people for many reasons having nothing to do with the person's sanity is a widespread practice, and has been going on, worldwide, for many, many years, everywhere!

Very often, in domestic disputes, in cases where an individual is wealthy and ruthless family members are trying to steal money from him, a psychiatrist who is greedy, will agree to denounce the victim as mentally incompetent, and therefore unable to manage his money, and the victim is either committed to a mental hospital, or jail, and will face years of phony hearings, phony charges, etc. while his life and his rights go away.

Horrible! Unreal! Rare! No, very real.

I asked Dr. Szasz to send me some lawyer's names, and he did.

I selected a woman attorney here in New York, with whom Dr. Szasz had worked.

Gene Ann Condon agreed to be my attorney when she learned of Dr. Szasz's recommendation.

She designed an approach to the Federal Courts, seeking my 14th amendment rights and this began a new nightmare.

Judge Anthony Travia heard our brief and a few days later, dismissed the case.

Gene Ann then appealed to the Second Circuit for relief, and this court sent the case back to Judge Travia, to re-hear the case he had just thrown out.

A judicial dirty trick going on. This is how plaintiffs get beaten down.

Why would a judge who had just been over-ruled by the higher court react favorably and impartially to the same brief he had just dismissed? Of course, he wouldn't.

Then Judge Travia resigned! How fortunate. My case was then re-assigned to a different judge – Judge Orin Judd –

We were very lucky to get him, since Gene Ann told me he was known for his compassion towards plaintiffs and his visits to prisons during Christmas holidays, to check on conditions there.

We met with Judge Judd and he said that he would hear my case, and we did not need a jury trial.

But fate stepped in again, but this time a tragic twist threw things into turmoil again. Judge Judd died suddenly.

It seems that no judge wants more cases added to his already crowded calendar. They'll do anything to prevent new cases being added to their lists, but decisions have to be made and thus I wound up on Judge Thomas Platt's plate.

Gene Ann conferred with him, and also told me that she was planning to retire in a few months and she wanted Platt to get busy and render a decision.

She told Judge Platt that too much time had already been wasted, and Ms. Newman's case must be ruled on, now.

Judge Platt promised Gene Ann that he would definitely hear my case and render his decision, and told her to make sure Ms. Newman's financial records for the period 1971-1975 be presented to him.

Gene Ann flew to County Mayo in Ireland, thinking all would go well.

She also told John Lombard and me that her friend, Attorney Rita Hayman, had agreed to await Judge Platt's decision, and to implement it and make sure all went well.

Well, dear reader, Attorney Hayman called me to come to collect my file and John Lombard's, also, (as Gene Ann was also acting as John's lawyer) because she didn't have time for this. She said she needed to attend to her own cases.

Talk about betrayal! Talk about honor! Disgusting! Unprofessional!

I called Gene Ann in Ireland, and she said to go ahead and seek another attorney to carry on. She did not express any anger towards Attorney Hayman. But I was upset, and John and I agreed to report Attorney Hayman's breaking her promise to Gene Ann, thus leaving us, the plaintiffs, without legal help, to the Bar Association.

The Bar contacted Rita Hayman.

She said she did nothing wrong.

The Bar contacted us and cleared her of any wrongdoing. Case closed!

Meanwhile, I was trying every means available to a victim to get the story out.

We called the papers and asked the reporters to write about the horrors of forced psychiatric exams used to silence and ruin teachers at the Board of Ed. and with the Teachers' Union (UFT) in total compliance.

We were promised that the paper would look into the complaint; the promise was broken.

We printed up flyers about the Board's Gulag Machinery and gave them out, in front of bookstores, libraries and fairs and handed out our leaflets to people as they strolled by.

Nothing but silence ensued!

We became members and activists in a recently formed group of angry teachers who were filing suit against some high school principals who were abusing their teachers.

This group, Teachers United For Fair Treatment, organized by a feisty history teacher at Seward Park H.S., Mary Macaulay, was using Attorney Joan Goldberg to plead their cases.

I was impressed with Joan Goldberg, and hired her to pursue my case.

She wrote briefs; she called Platt's office many times and was told that Judge Platt was now awaiting a decision on the Monell case, which dealt with pay issues on pregnancy leaves.

Then a bombshell occurred. I could hardly believe it. Can you, dear reader, believe it?

Judge Platt threw my case out in June, months before the Monell came down, from the US Supreme Court. (November)

Another broken promise occurred.

There was nothing Joan could do except try to get a Federal jury trial, to settle my case.

So more briefs written and ignored!

Back into the judicial refrigerator!

Meanwhile, before Gene Ann had left, she urged John Lombard and me to appeal to the Social Security Administration to get copies of our medical report (the forced ones that were being withheld from us) claiming that our employer said we were mentally disabled, and I was saying I was not ill, and was awaiting a Federal trial to clear my name, and get rid of whatever labels had been fastened to me.

So I followed Gene Anne's advice and sent off a request to the Social Security office in Washington, DC, requesting that they secure copies of my medical reports that Dr. Liebowitz and Dr. Pool, the Boards' were not releasing, despite all my requests for them to send their doctor's reports on me, to my own doctors.

Here's where George Orwell, the famous author of "Animal Farm" and "1984" enters the picture, with his position that "Big Brother" is watching, is ever-present in every citizen's affairs.

The letter from the Social Security Administration said that Miss Newman should not be shown these reports, as these reports might interfere with her medical management.

Unbelievable! Shocking!

This letter was in the files that Gene Ann had given to Attorney Hayman. She had never mentioned this letter to me.

Jerome J. Feiner, administrative law judge, wrote to Dr. Pool, and said her letter to the Social Security Bureau of Disability Insurance was inadequate. Dr. Pool was directed to send the actual reports on me to the bureau, and not the conclusory summary that Dr. Pool had submitted.

Attached is a copy of Dr. Pool's letter which slanders me, damages me, and lies about me. She had never spoken to me, examined me, or anything, yet she submits this letter to Social Security as though I was her private patient, whom she had recently seen. This woman is a liar, a criminal.

This was 1976 now, and the Freedom of Information act was passed, and acting upon its power, Gene was able to get the actual Medical reports on me, issued by Dr. Liebowitz.

Dr. Liebowitz had been telling the office of Professional Conduct in Albany, that I was a very seriously ill woman, passive aggressive, hypomanic, explosive, and that I was unfit to be in a classroom.

This from a doctor who <u>never</u> met me, nor spoke to me, nor examined me.

Outrageous! Sickening! Yes, but true.

Joan filed many briefs designed to get a Federal judge and a jury to hear the case.

But the calendar was very crowded and all the sitting Federal judges had full caseloads.

An emergency situation was building up. Washington was becoming concerned at the increasing backlog of civil cases in New York.

Time ticked by, day after day, week after week, month after month, year after year, and the unbearable frustration continued to build up, within me.

My attorney continued to try to get the case before the Federal Court and she was continually rebuffed.

However, one day Joan was able to secure a 15 minute hearing before 3 judges. The Board of Ed.'s attorneys also are granted the same time frame, and the sitting judges then render their decision, which would, if favorable, move my case to the court's calendar more quickly.

[attach picture (letter) "01" here]

We were now in the <u>ninth</u> year of the case, and surely, I thought, the judges sitting up there would be able to see and hear and feel the injustice of the whole matter before them.

Joan spoke eloquently, reasonably, as she pleaded for justice for me, stating my exemplary record, my almost-perfect attendance record beyond my teaching duties, such as coaching, reviewing of incoming students' health files, arranging for guest speakers for our hygiene program, etc. and that continued non-action by the court was unjust, unfair and unwarranted, and that Miss Newman's life and career were already badly damaged.

The judges listened, and then the court's alarm clock rang, and the 15 minutes allotted to us ended.

The court clerk then called the Board's attorney to the front of the room, and asked him to state his case.

Well, dear reader, prepare yourself for the next outrage coming up right now. Ready? Here goes!

The Board's representative was a City Corporation Counsels' department attorney named Kevin Sheridan.

He stood up and told the court that he had no brief to present, as he had been busy with other matters, and <u>did not have time</u> to prepare a position paper.

This was the <u>ninth</u> year that we were in, now, and he was saying that he had <u>no time</u> to get ready.

He claimed that other attorneys had the case before he was assigned and that he <u>absolutely</u> needed more time to present the required 15 minute presentation.

Joan argued that this was unfair, but she was immediately silenced.

The 3 judges up there, looking solemn and stonefaced, asked Attorney Sheridan how much more time he needed, and Sheridan settled for a few months.

They granted the delay asked for and we left the courtroom.

I felt tears coming, and nausea and anger, all at once.

Joan comforted me as best she could, and we left the Foley Square building and headed for the nearest coffee shop.

Joan explained to me that she would continue to try to get us on the current court calendar; that as soon as Sheridan sent in or personally came into the court with his 15 minute argument, she would press her demand for a speedy trial.

She expressed, in the usual lawyer-ly kind of way, with a minimum of any personal emotionalism, that the Board's statement of not being ready to present a brief, in the 9th year of the case, was ridiculous, ludicrous, but we would have to wait until Sheridan's brief was presented.

I went home, to a private grieving.

And, a few months later, the court received a "letter brief" from Attorney Sheridan, filled with the Board's insistence about this teacher's mental unfitness, and blah, blah, blah. Noting new here, just the same lies, presented once again, in order to further delay outcome…

But, luckily for me, the Federal Court judges in Washington, became even more concerned that the increasing backlog of unheard civil cases in New York was a very serious problem and they came up with the following solution: to make more judges available to hear the cases, judges at the <u>magistrate level</u> were being empowered to hear the stalled cases, in order to move things along. This order was to begin, immediately.

. . . .

So, my attorney, ready for anything, immediately filed again, for my case to be heard, and we did get Magistrate A.S. Chrein to hear my case.

But, first a jury had to be impaneled.

When the judge addressed the assembled pool of would-be jurors, he told them this was a case of a mentally-ill teacher trying to be re-instated to her position, and before he uttered another falsehood, I jumped up an sputtered out that a teacher who had been placed on an <u>involuntary</u> leave of absence because of a principal's charges that she was behaving in a bizarre fashion and was incompetent to be a teacher, etc, ad nauseum, this was false.

I explained that I was a teacher unfairly targeted as a mentally ill woman, and was placed on an involuntary leave of absence, despite my doctor's reports that I was mentally fit.

The judge told Joan to keep me quiet, and I sat down, to hear him correct his original statement to the assembled jury pool.

Eventually, 6 people were selected to be the jurors and my case, US73civ473, was re-opened to be heard, before a jury.

The trial began on <u>Dec. 14, 1980</u> and lasted till Dec. 24, 1980.

It was a 10 day trial, during which the chief cannibalizers of me, Principal David Gordon, Dr. Naomi Pool, and Dr. Morris Isenberg were questioned as to why they found me to be suddenly unfit, even though my teaching skills and accomplishments were unquestionably good!

Several teachers from my dept. testified that I was a terrible person, yelling and screaming at assisting teachers and at her students.

Several students testified that they didn't want to write nasty letters about me, but were enticed to do so, by promise of special programs, etc.

Judge Chrein was paying very close attention to every word uttered by these witnesses.

When Dr. Isenberg told the jury that even though he only saw Miss Newman for a very few moments, he could see that I was ill, and rattled off the psychiatric jargon disguised as facts.

Judge Chrein asked Dr. Isenberg how he could possibly make such decisions, in such a short time, and especially since Miss Newman had a practically impeccable record.

This pompous psychiatrist then testified that he was a <u>very good doctor</u>, and when he examined soldiers he could detect who was ill or homosexual or whatever in a very few minutes.

Judge Chrein said he had heard enough from this doctor, and closed the testimony section of the trial, as he asked Dr. Isenberg if the Board of Ed's medical division doctors, Liebowitz and Pool had told him what to write about Newman in order to make sure she'd be labeled as "unfit".

Dr. Isenberg's sputtering and shifting in his seat and failure to deny this presumptive statement by the judge made an impression on the jury, too. These 6 never missed a day or asked to be excused for personal reasons, despite the fact that this trial was being heard just before the Christmas – New Years' holiday.

Judge Chrein sequestered the jury into the jurors' room, and closed the case.

He said he would await the jury's decision.

My sister, Carolyn, hugged me as we left the courtroom for lunch, and gave me emotional support all through the 10 days.

My attorney felt confident, and told me that she felt the jury would rule for me.

Her attitude, was, as usual, let's wait and see......

We all returned to the courtroom, to hear the jury, <u>unanimously</u>, rule in my favor.

They ordered the psychiatric labels expunged from my records.

They ordered my sick days bank restored.

They pointed their fingers at the Boards' and the U.F.T's attorneys sitting in a nearby corner, and denounced the Gulag tactics being used in NYC, USA, and said that they must stop, now, once and for all.

They ordered me back to school, at once.

The jurors came up to me, as the courtroom, emptied and wished me luck.

Joan was happy, and expressed her view that pretty soon, I'd be back in school, teaching once again.

My sister and Joan and I stopped for a cup of coffee, and then Joan left, telling us that she would keep me posted on any new developments, and told me to relax, and wait.

....

Dear reader, after wading through this book of atrocities committed against an ordinary high school teacher, by top-level administrators and lawyers and licensed NY doctors, you may want to close the book, and discuss it with friends and family and any lawyers you may know.

You may be relieved of reading any further.

Well, sorry to tell you this, but there's more. Here goes! I might add here that I was shocked when Joan called to tell me that the Board's lawyers wanted me to be examined by their psychiatrist, to see if I was fit, now, in 1980, to resume teaching.

The influence here was that after all I had been put through (by them) I might be unfit now and in need of psychiatric care.

Joan forbade this and told the Board that Miss Newman was fine, fit and eager to get back to work, now, after all this.

Joan agreed to a physical exam, however; so we went down to the Medical Division for a routine physical.

As soon as we identified ourselves, the stocky woman doctor told Joan she had to remain outside the exam room. Joan told this doctor that the law permitted a teacher in Miss Newman's position to have a witness.

The doctor balked, and was insistent that Joan stay outside the room.

A compromise was reached. Joan stood at the rear of the room, while this doctor whispered in my ear and mumbled something about why the principal at Far Rockaway H.S. went after me.

I gasped! I sputtered to her, "How dare you question me about this? This happened 10 years ago. They told you to harass me, right?"

Joan came running up, and told me to leave immediately. As I attempted to exit, the doctor threatened Joan with arrest.

Two guards came running up to us, and Joan stared them down and told the doctor that she would report this doctor to the city's lawyers.

Joan rushed me out, into the elevator, and into a nearby coffee shop.

She called the Corporation Counsels' office and later informed me that the doctor's exam was OK (never completed) and I could report to Forest Hills H.S. on the first school day in Sept. 1981 –

Thus, I began and served a five year period, successfully; No complaints!

I enjoyed teaching at Forest Hills H.S. and received Satisfactory ratings for my 5 year stay. ~

Now, in closing, I'd like to add a few facts, questions and statements, designed to have you, the reader, focus in on the entrenched horrors going on, under your noses, and paid for with your tax dollars!!!

Fact: In the UFT contract, there is a 4 step agreement, in the grievance area: 1 – the aggrieved teacher files a complaint <u>against</u> the

> 1) principal and waits for a hearing:
> Then, it turns out that the <u>principal</u>
> is also the <u>hearing officer</u>. The
> perpetrator is also the judge!

Believe it or not, its' the truth, and in all the contracts since 1970 the same clauses appear!

> 2) I had <u>9</u> grievance hearings a la the UFT contract.
> I was denied in all of them.
> How can this be?

3) Along my way I met a police officer, Charles Leahy, who blew the whistle on police dept. practices that affected him. He was subjected to the forced psychiatric exams and constant harassment and denials that I received! I thank him for his constancy, his keeping me in close touch with his nightmare and his efforts to inform the public of the police "quota system", which the police denied!

4) Along my way, I met Acquilla Fitzgerald, a feisty Dept. of Transportation employee, in Washington, D.C. who had filed numerous complaints against her employees.

She was never promoted. She was always being sent for coffee and donuts and being humiliated. She appealed to many Congressmen on the hill and got nowhere.

Being a black woman was part of her problem.

I commend her for her many years of striving to clean-up the unfair, racist practices in her agency. Her efforts did make a difference.

5) We never knew we were on a blacklist at the Board of Ed. Apparently my file number was on it for 9 years – 144709.

When I complained to Judge Platt about the blacklist, he said in his decision, that there was no blacklist......but even if there was one, no one knew about it except for the fact that Miss Newman keeps talking about one.

I could go on and on and search my memory bank for many, many other occurrences that were heaped on me, and others.

I must add that reporter Jack Anderson, in Washington, DC wrote quite a few excellent articles on the plight of whistleblowers at this time.

And lastly, Congressman Gladys Spellman was showing interest in the use of unconstitutional "forced psychiatric exams" on Federal employees. She surmised that employees' right to due process was being squelched and ignored, and she set out to correct this horror. Unfortunately, she died, at this time!

My apologies to any person I should have included in this expose and warm thanks to you, the readers, for reading this book. I hope you will act on your newly-learned knowledge! You can stop all this!

I also wish to thank the 2 attorneys who really won this case for me – Gene Ann Cordon, who began my Federal case, and Joan Goldberg who saw the case through to the end – They both were wonderful. They both really did everything possible to win this case.

Francine Newman

About the Author

   Francine Newman grew up in Laurelton, Queens, the daughter of a local doctor. She received a B.A. from Hunter College and an M.A. from Teachers' College, Columbia University. She traveled to Europe, Japan, and East and West Africa to study education and health practices as well as governments and history to earn graduate credits. She traveled with Syracuse University and Howard University as well as private travel groups.

   She taught twenty-nine years of high school health education and physical education. She worked as a substitute teacher at Andrew Jackson High School, John Adams High School, and Far Rockaway High School, all in Queens, and as fulltime teacher at JHS210 in Brooklyn and Far Rockaway High School and Forest Hills High School in Queens.

www.ingramcontent.com/pod-product-compliance
Lightning Source LLC
Chambersburg PA
CBHW030311290526
45785CB00001B/302